TABLE OF CONTENTS

CHAPTER 1: INTRODUCTION

"I say to you: that we are in a battle, and that more than half of this battle is taking place in the battlefield of the media. And that we are in a media battle in a race for the hearts and minds," [1] *Ayman al-Zawahiri, intercepted letter to Abu Musab al-Zarqawi, 9 July 2005.*

Over two hundred years ago, Carl Von Clausewitz, introduced his paradoxical trinity of the state, the military, and the people, and how the three influence the governance of a nation.[2] Throughout time, people's passion and the human dimension seem to influence everything relating to the government and military affairs. Whether the public supports a government's decision to wage war in order to protect the Nation's interest or to protest the same government's desire to change social systems, the collective voice of the people can quickly change the direction of a nation. With the influence of the public in mind, those that efficiently inform the public often gain support for their cause. Additionally, as those providing information continue to see their influence and power grow in the 21st century information environment, joint forces must continue to improve their military-media relationship in order to communicate their narrative effectively to all stakeholders. For the purpose of this paper, the narrative is defined as the open, timely, and accurate communication with domestic and international citizens, political leaders, and the news media that not only informs but also contributes to the achievement and support of all military objectives.[3]

The joint forces must assume a more proactive role in educating their leaders writ large in order to sustain the current favorable public support and meet the demands of a

---

[1] Thomas F. Metz, Mark W. Garrett, James E. Hutton, and Timothy W. Bush, "Massing Effects in the Information Domain: A Case Study in Aggressive Information Operations," *Military Review* 86 (May-June 2006): 2.

[2] Carl Von Clausewitz, *On War*, ed. Michael Howard and Peter Paret (New Jeresy: Princeton University Press, 1976), 100.

[3] U.S. Joint Chiefs of Staff, Public Affairs, *Joint Publication 3-61* (Washington DC: Joint Chiefs of Staff, August 25, 2010), vii-I-7.

dynamic and uncertain operating environment. In order to sustain and continue to foster constituent support for military operations, the joint forces must continue to produce a quality narrative. A method to achieve these goals of improved interaction with the environment and stakeholders, produce an effective narrative, and cultivate the military-media relationship is through education. Currently the levels of education throughout the Joint Professional Military Education (JPME) structure do not sufficiently prioritize or address how to deliver a timely, accurate, and transparent narrative through a cooperative relationship between two organizations with different goals and values.

Because of this mismatch, the author purports a holistic look at the Joint Professional Military Education system is needed to get to the solution. All military leaders should receive more education in fostering the military-media relationship. This education, spanning a military member's career, should focus on building better interpersonal relationships with the media and confidently articulating the military's narrative while balancing an environment influenced greatly by mass media and adversary actions. The goal of this holistic education is to ingrain a joint force with the ability to thrive within a dynamic information environment and articulate a timely, accurate, and transparent military narrative that informs the American public and sustains support and trust for future military operations.

Currently, there is much rhetoric surrounding the importance of effectively communicating and operating with the mass media in order to sustain support for military operations through the narrative. While some services attempt to train and educate their leaders in managing the narrative, the overall education afforded to military leaders writ large remains insufficient to meet the growing demands of the information environment.

Although senior leaders stress education and fostering a working military-media relationship, this emphasis of understanding is not reaching the lowest levels within the force. The 21st century information environment is very dynamic and complex. This complexity continues to grow as both media and individuals continue to shape policy and public opinion. Additionally, the advances in communication technologies, the competitive 24/7 news cycle, a growing public appetite for information, and the flattening of communications (social media and email) quickly builds support and adds voice to obscure causes and creates a complex environment in which military leaders must understand and adapt to in order to achieve military objectives. As such, military leaders at all levels must better prepare themselves and their units to ensure a timely, accurate, and transparent narrative reaches the public.

As the global environment continues to evolve, the military will continue to demonstrate a relevant and valuable position within society. However, the military cannot take its current position or approval rating for granted. It must continue to evolve and not allow current policy and resourcing challenges to return its position or prestige to the misunderstanding and mistrust reminiscent of the Vietnam Era. As the global effects of information disseminated through the mass media (as defined as broadcast, on-line, and social media outlets) continue to challenge leaders, the joint force must adapt, continue to learn, and apply the lessons of the past. This paper uses a gambit of information from document research to interviews to advocate for a more holistic military leader education in communicating the military's narrative successfully within a complex information environment. This paper analyzes the type and effects of select historical case studies involving military-media relationships and then draws out the critical utility of these relationships for today's environment. After demonstrating a need for improving education, the author advocates for a greater prioritization and incorporation of military-media relations and narrative building education throughout the joint force. Increasing the prioritization of building the military-media relationship and effective communication will build capacity in all leaders to thrive in the current operating environment while sustaining public support for national goals.

The current chapter introduces the reader to the reason for this analysis on the military-media relationship and the influential power of the media. It establishes the outline for how the author plans to build a case for enhanced education in order to producing a timely, accurate, and transparent narrative while effectively fostering a productive relationship with the media. Chapter two provides a historical examination of major military–media relationships from Vietnam until current operations. Because of the scope of the paper, the author examines history starting from the most contentious and influential military-media period, the Vietnam War. This chapter evaluates periods of history using a framework that compares overall feelings and effectiveness of different military-media relationships, select examples contributing to that period, the lessons observed, and then how that period contributed to other periods of history.

Chapter three examines the current operating environment shared by both the military and media. It explores current threats and the goals, values, and struggles of the two organizations. Because of this comparison, the reader will see how both the media and military fight for the narrative, while operating within a complex and changing information environment full of monetary incentives, requirements to sustain support, and satisfies the demands the 24/7 news cycle. Chapter three concludes by establishing the framework for understanding the complexity of the environment. After exploring current threats and environmental factors, chapter four uses a Rogerian approach to advocate for a more holistic education system.[4] Through this approach, the author examines the positions of both the military and the media, their importance within society, and then challenges military leaders to provide greater opportunities for education, training, and fostering enduring military-media relationships. Chapter four concludes by recommending a feasible solution focused on joint education from initial entry into the military to higher-level education in order to better prepare and comprehensively shape military leaders to operate in the 21st century information environment. Chapter five summarizes this paper with an analysis of the military-media relationship and the need to improve the joint forces through education. By incorporating and redefining education in regards to the military-media relationships, joint forces writ large can better achieve the goals of advancing the military's narrative through a cooperative and understanding military-media relationship and sustain the current high level of support demonstrated by the American public for the U.S. Armed Forces.

---

[4] A Rogerian Approach presents both views of an argument. After which an author explains his position and tries to find the common ground between two issues. This approach is contrary to the winner-loser argument normally presented.

CHAPTER 2: HISTORY OF THE MILITARY-MEDIA RELATIONSHIP

"It is in vain that the voice of the press, of public meetings, of formal deputations, is heard imploring the President to give efficiency to his administration. The instruction of the people is needed [sic]; and that must be given at the ballot box. We have reached that stage of political crisis wherein our position resembles that of the British Parliament, when a revolution of political opinion dictates a change of ministry and a modification of governmental policy."[1]

The military-media relationship is not a new phenomenon plaguing only the contemporary joint force. The thirst for information and the desire to quench it follows warring armies throughout history like the smell of death. Whether receiving information from printed sources or from images, the desire for information continues to expand and influence society. For example, Thucydides provides an early example of the influence and dangers of information in his written diaries describing the 431 B.C. Peloponnesian Wars and how "people are inclined to accept all stories in an uncritical way."[2] Similarly, the 17th Century naval historical drawings of Willem van de Velde the Elder informed kings and served as an academic basis for teaching about warfare.[3] These examples illustrate the numerous formats of information and their ability to influence not only political and military leaders but also society. As the influence of information continues to grow, because of increased demand and improved technologies, the need for deeper study and appreciation of those controlling the information and the narrative continues to serve as an essential and important undertaking of the joint force.

As such, this chapter provides a historical perspective in order to provide a basic understanding of the military-media relationship and its effects on communicating to the

---

[1] *The Richmond Daily Dispatch*, "The Political Uprising at the North," *The Richmond Daily Dispatch,* September 23, 1862.

[2] Thucydides, *History of the Peloponnesian War*, trans. Rex Warner (New York: Penguin Group, 1972), 46.

[3] The National Gallery, *Willem van de Velde,*. London. http://www.nationalgallery.org.uk/artists/willem-van-de-velde. (accessed September 11, 2013).

public. This paper compares five decades of America at war through the lenses of the role of the media, feelings surrounding the military-media relationship, and the enduring effects of those roles and feelings on future conflicts. This historical examination will highlight periods of mistrust and disdain, the effect of those feelings on the narrative and public opinion, the confusion created by the polar opposite objectives of both the military and media, and concludes with current improved military-media relations facilitated by military leaders committed to learning from history, understanding the effects of information, and rebuilding trust with the media. This paper begins its analysis with the Vietnam Conflict – the period often associated with the most negative military-media relationships and shaping generations of military leaders.

Vietnam

"If I had my choice I would kill every reporter in the world, but I am sure we would be getting reports from Hell before breakfast."[4]- General William Tecumseh Sherman

The Vietnam conflict created the backdrop in which ambiguous political policy, both international and domestic, contributed to the loss of military credibility, and a shift to critical journalism. The global events that occurred between 1960 and 1970 created an environment forcing political leaders and the media to prioritize which crisis they would address and focus on first. Events like the Bay of Pigs and Space Race of 1961, the Cuban Missile Crisis and death of Marilyn Monroe in 1962, and the 1963 assassination of President Kennedy and the Civil Rights Movement made prioritizing of coverage and policy difficult. As Hallin, the author of *The Media, the War in Vietnam, and Political Support*, explained in an article refuting the claim of an oppositional media, the media did

---

[4] Dennis McGinn and William French, "Basic Media Training" inbriefing presentation for the Washington Navy Yard Recovery, email to author, November 8, 2013.

7

shift to more objective and critical coverage, rather than oppositional coverage, because

of domestic dissent and world events.[5] Because of the difficulty in prioritizing by both

the Kennedy Administration and media executives, early reports from reporters like

Homer Bigart of the New York *Times,* Malcolm Browne of the *Associated Press,* and

Francois Sully of *Newsweek*, although objective, seemed to challenge policies and reports

coming from "official" press conferences.[6] As a result, policies seemed ambiguous and

created the perception of mistrust.

Until 1965, the Vietnam press corps possessed unlimited access to the battlefield,

a relatively sporadic but supportive relationship with the military and both the Kennedy

and Johnson Administrations, and tried to report in support U.S. actions in Vietnam. The

1968 Tet offensive however served as the catalyst of the media's mistrust of the military

and the military's hostile relationship towards the media. The events unfolding after

1968 would negatively influence the military-media relationship for over four decades.

The Vietnam conflicts demonstrates a period in history in which extenuating

environmental factors adversely affected the perceptions of the press, the military, and a

nation. The circumstances surrounding Vietnam shows the military practitioner how

credibility, ambiguous international and domestic policy, an uncertain and unstable

global environment, conflicting organization objectives, increasing media influence, and

improved technology can greatly influence public opinion and national policy.

The decline of credibility and trust started as political leaders placed Vietnam on

the back burner and did not provide a clear national strategy. At the onset of Vietnam

[5] Daniel C. Hallin, "The Media, the War in Vietnam, and Political Support: A Critique of the Thesis of an Oppositional Media," *Journal of Politics* 46:1 (February 1984), 11-19.

[6] William M. Hammond, *Reporting Vietnam: Media and Military at War* (Kansas: University Press of Kansas, 1998), 1.

coverage, the media enjoyed open access to soldiers and government officials that enabled "ground truth" reporting. These initial relationships enabled journalists to see the execution of operations firsthand and the corrupt actions of the Diem Regime. But when these firsthand reports ran contrary to official messaging and stories reported in the continental U.S., perceptions and support of Vietnam changed for the worst. The credibility, trust, and actions of Homer Bigart, John Paul Vann, Robert S. McNamara, and Generals Harkins and Westmoreland illustrate how these traits will influence relationships and public opinion. Bigart and Vann highlight positive results of maintaining credibility and trust, while the others do not. In Homer Bigart's case, by successfully reporting in the Pacific during World War II, the Palestine War, Korea, Algeria, and the Middle East, Bigart established relationships and a resume that provided authority to his stories. His experience provided context to his reporting and enabled him to question the actions of government and military officials with confidence.[7]

Similarly, Lieutenant Colonel Paul Vann demonstrates the military example of possible positive outcomes of trust and credibility on maintaining a good military-media relationship. During his tour, Vann built natural relationships, welcomed reporters, and encouraged his subordinates to share information with vetted reporters. Prior to any access, Vann reviewed credentials and expected reporters to share in the hardship and prove themselves in the field.[8] An excellent example of Vann's relationship with the press occurred during the January 1963 Battle of Ap Bac. During this battle, Vann and his reporters provided real-time assessments and accurate accounts of that battle. Although those reports ran contrary to "official" reports from General Harkins and his

---

[7] Peter Braestrup, *Big Story* (Colorado: Westview Press, 1977), 5-6.
[8] Neil Sheehan, *A Bright Shining Lie* (New York: Random House, 1988), 270.

staff, the media knew they could trust Vann's accounts over official reports. Although considered a maverick by military leaders, Vann's credibility and trust endeared him to the press and fostered a successful military-media relationship. While Bigart and Vann's examples demonstrate positive actions in maintaining credibility and trust, the actions of McNamara, Harkins, and Westmoreland demonstrate the opposite.

Robert S. McNamara and Generals Harkins and Westmoreland lost credibility not only for themselves but also within their organizations. During the spring of 1962, tension and mistrust started to increase between correspondents, the Kennedy Administration, and the military. A 1962 visit to Vietnam and speech by Secretary McNamara illustrated the building apprehension and mistrust between the media and the government. McNamara baffled reporters when he reported the resounding success within Vietnam after only spending less than two days in country. Mistrust surfaced when, during a press conference prior to his departure, the Secretary stated, "he was tremendously encouraged by developments and the Vietnamese people had more security"[9] and continued that "[he'd] seen nothing but progress and hopeful indications of further progress in the future."[10] When asked for confirmation of his findings by Neil Sheehan, McNamara replied, "every quantitative measurement we have shows that we're winning this war."[11] This example highlights how predetermined national strategy and a failure to understand or adapt to ground truth created ambiguity and the conditions for journalists to question and become critical. This predetermined outcome reflected by McNamara and the administration also contributed to the decline of trust within the military. As military leaders operated in this political uncertainty, executed conflicting

---

[9] Braestrup, *Big Story*, 2.
[10] Sheehan, *A Bright Shining Lie*, 289-290.
[11] Ibid. 289-290.

national guidance, and supported multiple administrations, they would lose the trust of the media and the public.

General Harkins and the Battle of Ap Bac provides the first example of a senior military officer seen as disconnected and unreliable. Unlike the success demonstrated by Vann during the Battle of Ap Bac, this small battle in 1963 contributed to the decline of Harkins' credibility and the trust in the official narrative. Soon after the Viet Cong's 514th Battalion defeated the 7th South Vietnamese Division, Harkins explained to reporters (some just returning from the battle itself), that "we've got them in a trap and we're going to spring it in half an hour."[12] Whether unprepared or over confident, Harkins' failure to understand the environment and his audience contributed to the media's loss of confidence in Harkin's official reports. This battlefield summary coupled with earlier and future public affairs guidance led to a complete distrust of the military's narrative. For example, guidance issued first by the U.S. Information Agency and then the State and Defense Departments in 1962, "to curb the attacks and criticism of the South Vietnamese government and maximize cooperation without compromising security," laid the foundation for the perception of mistrust between the press and the military.[13]

Additionally, after Harkins' failed Ap Bac summary, both the Defense Department and U.S. Continental Army Command (CONARC) issued new guidance for:

> Personnel in South Vietnam to confine their conversations with reporters to areas of personnel responsibility and knowledge, avoid generalizations and to emphasize the positive aspects of your activities and avoid gratuitous criticism. Emphasize the feelings of achievement, the hopes for the future, instances of outstanding individual or unit performance and

---

[12] Ibid. 276.
[13] Hammond, *Reporting Vietnam,* 3.

optimism in general. But don't destroy your personal credibility by gilding the lily.[14]

This guidance proved too much to bear by the Vietnam press and relegated journalists to seek their facts from soldiers in the field or low-level government officials. Admittedly, the above guidance resembles contemporary approaches; however, at the time it contributed to a growing perception of wrongdoing, a perception that inflamed journalists, and corroded the media's relationship with the military and the government.

This antagonizing relationship in Vietnam coupled with President Johnson's request for his commanding general to sell and build support for the war also led to the demise of General Westmoreland and the further erosion of the military's credibility. Although gaining support in 1965, General Westmoreland would see his credibility and ability to execute operations in Vietnam destroyed after the 1968 Tet Offensive. Prior to this offensive, President Johnson ordered the Military Assistance Command, Vietnam (MACV) commander to build support for the war with both the media and the public. As Westmoreland followed orders, he did so without the mutual support of the executive and the legislative branches. An example of working at cross-purposes between the executive and legislative branches came during an April 1967 speaking engagement to the Associated Press Managing Editors' Association. Westmoreland created consternation among both reporters and Congress by explaining his perception of how negative reports and limited political support aided the enemy's efforts.[15] While this event may have contributed to the division between the military and the press, it would not compare to the two media engagements occurring later in 1967. During November 1967, Westmoreland tried to rally support when he addressed first the National Press Club and then the NBC

---

[14] Ibid, 11.
[15] Hammond, *Reporting Vietnam,* 100.

12

news program *Meet the Press*. During these engagements he explained great progress and how the "U.S. was gaining the upper hand and would begin to turn the fight and the security over to the South Vietnamese within two years," and although true, actual events at the time (Tet 1968) contradicted his claims of progress and destroyed his credibility.[16] After Tet, both the press and Congress saw him as an extension of the President's failed efforts in Vietnam and stopped listening and supporting his reports on the conduct of the war.

Although these leaders tried building support for the war, the ambiguous policies, the global events of the 60s and 70s, and the actions of the enemy discredited their attempts and created a climate of distrust. These trends coupled with the media's appetite and methods of reporting the Vietnam conflict continued to create hostilities between the media, the government, and the America people. The mistrust created from previous examples coupled with the advent of televised reporting and more vivid photojournalism enabled the media and the public to reshape opinion and policy the way they saw fit. The advancements in communications technology together with the complex environment enabled the media to extend its influence quickly and globally because of its ability to provide real-time observations of war and its atrocities.

The Vietnam conflict was the event that changed how the public saw and understood the coverage of warfare. The introduction of television and the advancement in photojournalism fulfilled the media's desire to profit, influence world opinion, and shape global understanding and policy. In addition to the influential effects of television, two photojournalism examples provide additional support in the media's ability to shape opinion and policy globally. The first example comes from a dramatic photograph

---

[16] Ibid, 106-107.

captured by *AP*'s Malcolm Browne in June 1963. In his picture, Browne captures the self-emulsification of a South Vietnamese Monk protesting the religious persecution of the Diem Regime; and in a little over 15 hours, the world saw photographic proof.[17] In addition to the new speed of dissemination, this example also demonstrates the influential nature of the media on a global scale. When the government ignored the protest of South Vietnamese monks, the monks turned to international journalist to convey their suffering to the world. Because of the severity and global dissemination of this one picture, the American public and the Kennedy Administration could see the brutality of the war and began to question their support and policies for Vietnam. As the *AP* explained, 50 years after the event, this one image so shocked President Kennedy that he immediately ordered a review of his policies dealing with Vietnam.[18] Like Browne, the General Loan picture captured by Eddie Adams provides an additional example of the profound and immediate influence of the media or a single person on public opinion.

In February 1968, the picture of General Loan, the chief of South Vietnam's National Police, executing a Viet Cong prisoner captured by Adams provides another example of the influence of a single image. This picture quickly circulated in American newspapers and showed the graphic brutality of war. It also demonstrated the importance of context and Thucydides' warning of the public's lack of desire to understand the full story or its context. Although Peter Arnett calls the picture a "brilliant piece of photography," he explains how Adams "never came to terms with the fact that the anti-

---

[17] Hammond, *Reporting Vietnam,* 9-11; Patrick Witty, "Malcolm Browne: The Story Behind the Burning Monk," *Time Lightbox,* August 28, 2012, http://lightbox.time.com/2012/08/28/malcolm-browne-the-story-behind-the-burning-monk/#1 (accessed November 19, 2013); and *Associated Press,* 50th Anniversary, "The Burning Monk: A Defining Moment Photographed by *AP*'s Malcolm Browne," June 2013, http://www.ap.org/explore/the-burning-monk/ (accessed November 19, 2013).
[18] Associated Press, "The Burning Monk."

war movement saw that picture as the photograph that proved that the American war effort was not worthy."[19] Although this picture aided antiwar movements when published by American newspapers, its initial purpose was to inform while balancing the atrocities of war. A New York *Times'* Front-page story illustrates this desire to balance information when they carried both Adam's picture with another *AP* picture capturing the desperation of a South Vietnamese officer carrying his dead child.[20] The pictures snapped by both Browne and Adams serve to demonstrate the speed and influential effects of the media on policy and public opinion. This influence coupled with the loss of military credibility and trust created the environment that continued to influence relationships for four decades.

The importance of Vietnam is not to encourage "how the media lost the war" attitude but to show the importance of credibility, trust, and the power of the media to influence. The media fulfilled its role and informed the American people during the Vietnam conflict but became affected by the environment in which it operated. The domestic issues, the internal fighting between Congress and the President, combined with a war that for the first time the American public witnessed in near real time contributed to the overall sentiment of this period. The speed and clarity of advancing communication mediums fostered a dynamic that continues to shape modern warfare, national objectives, and the military-media relationship.

Post-Vietnam and Rebuilding a Relationship: Grenada to the Desert

---

[19] Margot Adler, "The Vietnam War, Through Eddie Adams' Lens," *NPR.org*, March 24, 2009; and Charles Mohrs, "Street Clashes go on in Vietnam, Foe Still Holds Parts of the Cities," *New York Times*, February 2, 1968, 1, February 2, 1968. 1, http://search.proquest.com.ezproxy6.ndu.edu/docview/118305054/pageviewPDF?accountid=12686 (accessed November 19, 2013).

[20] Mohrs, *New York Times*, 1.

The aftermath of Vietnam left the military-media relationship in shambles. The military's blame of the media "losing the war" and the erosion of trust between both would influence the military-media relationship for decades to come. As the military struggled to rebuild and regain trust with America, and the media came to terms with their influence and greater role in society, leaders from both entities struggled to rebuild their relationship and apply the lessons learned from the Vietnam conflict. The conflicts of the 1980s and 1990s slowly initiated improvements in the military-media relationship when both sides started to understand one another goals, reform their interaction, and adapt to a new environment enhanced by technology. From Grenada, 1983, where the media had no access, to the Gulf War, 1991, where the military controlled access and enforced rigid guidelines, both groups emerged with greater understanding, appreciation, and acceptance of each other.

The military learned several lessons from Vietnam while the media forgot their lessons. The military learned to "keep wars short and keep the news media completely controlled in the opening days of the engagement" while the media failed to learn "to never again look the other way or accept at face value official civil and military claims without careful examination."[21] While the media wrestled to understand their new ability to rapidly inform, influence, and profit from information, the military slowly struggled to learn how to balance operational security with producing a narrative that informed a nation (while understanding the media's desire for free flowing information and access).[22] Building from the lessons of Vietnam, the military denied access to Grenada

---

[21] Ben H. Bagdikian, "Forward" in John R. Macarthur, *Second Front, Censorship and Propaganda in the Gulf War* (California: University of California Press, 1992), xv.
[22] Judith R. Baroody, *Media Access and the Military: The Case of the Gulf War* (Maryland: University Press of America, 1998), viii.

until well after the most newsworthy stories passed. As a result, the media arrived days later and then were subjected to military briefings and military escorts.[23] Although the military claimed victory on the media front, the events of Grenada only served to enrage both national and local journalists and further exacerbated relationships. The outrage from Grenada grew as national outlets, using satellite capabilities and television, started to compete with local journalists and their newfound parity using technologies like portable video cameras.[24] This change in the information environment would hinder military interaction with the media and call for change.

The media's outrage and the military's inability to maximize greater technology; however, led to military media operations reform and better understanding by both the military and media. In the wake of Grenada, two studies emerged that made recommendations on how to improve relations while achieving organizational goals. The Chairman of the Joint Chiefs of Staff, General John W. Vessey, Jr., ordered the first study and charged Major General (retired) Winant Sidle to lead it. The "Sidle Commission" recommended eight ways to improve the military-media relationship. These recommendations included: 1) conduct public affairs planning concurrently with operational planning, 2) provide longer lead times and create larger media pools when it is evident that pools will provide the earliest access to military operations, 3) Secretary of Defense maintain a list of accredited journalists, 4) have voluntary compliance with security guidelines and to have few and previously agreed upon rules, 5) dedicate personnel to assist correspondents with equipment and public affairs operations, 6) account for communication required to cover the conflict, 7) provide required

---

[23] Ibid, 45 and 63.
[24] Baroody, *Media Access*, 18.

transportation, and 8) continue to conduct meetings between the Defense Department and media organizations in the interim.[25] Similarly, the independent Twentieth Century Fund Task Force on the Military and the Media asserted that the denial of access was unprecedented, a greater need for access between DoD and journalists was required, and for the military to place greater importance on public affairs officers.[26] Although constrained by time, the DoD tried to learn from past mistakes as the Panama invasion unfolded in December 1989. As the military attempted to adhere to earlier recommendations, those attempts fell short as reporters still arrived late and failed to conduct timely reporting on the current situation.[27] While Panama demonstrated marginal military improvement, the liberation of Kuwait forever changed the struggle between access, security, and the requirement to inform the American public.

Operations Desert Shield and Storm (August 1990 to March 1991) serves as a military victory in the military-media relationship saga. Although military leaders demonstrated the ability to conduct joint planning with the media, they soon realized the Gulf War served as the last time for military control of media access and information dissemination. The lead up and execution of this conflict demonstrates the ability of the two entities to plan together. It also balanced the military's desire to control the media and protect operational planning with the media's short attention span and need the need to earn a profit. The combined planning of the Gulf War better adhered with the Sidle and the Twentieth Century panels but still proved controversial based on external factors; for example, Saudi Arabian sovereignty and global media opinions. While touted as the

---

[25] Kelly Cecil and Mark Sullivan, *Media War Coverage and Pentagon Policy, Policy Analysis Exercise,* submitted to the Honorable J. Daniel Howard, Assistant Secretary of Defense (Public Policy) (Massachusetts: Harvard University 1989), 41-43; and Baroody, *Media Access,* 65.
[26] Baroody, *Media Access,* 65-66.
[27] Ibid, 68.

best war coverage in history by Pete Williams, the then Assistant Secretary of Defense for Public Affairs, the Gulf War provides many lessons for both military and media professionals.[28] In regards to planning and preparing for the Gulf War, the media had to plan with the Defense Department just to gain access into Saudi Arabia, as Saudis did not desire western journalists in their country.[29] This need to consult and plan with DoD contributed to resolving access issues and development of press pool rules prior to hostilities. These prior negotiations also illustrate the power of media executives and their need to find common ground in order to profit and achieve stakeholder interests.

After obtaining access, media executives continued to work DoD officials on defining ground rules and coordinating logistical support. In so doing, Williams claimed the Defense Department used history to shape ground rules that "were not intended to prevent journalists from reporting on incidents that might embarrass the military or to make military operations look sanitized. Instead, they were intended simply and solely to prevent publication of details that could jeopardize a military operation or endanger the lives of U.S. troops."[30] Additionally, he claimed the rules and pools "got reporters out to see the action, guaranteed that Americans at home got reports from the scene of the action, and allowed the military to accommodate a reasonable number of journalists without overwhelming the units that were fighting the enemy."[31] As the military proclaimed success, the media disagreed and argued over their inability to cover the Gulf War adequately. While "beat" journalists disapproved of the coverage arrangements,

---

[28] Pete Williams, "Military, Media and Manipulation," *The Washington Post,* March 17, 1991, D1-D4, http://search.proquest.com.ezproxy6.ndu.edu/docview/140385452?accountid=12686 (accessed October 2, 2013).

[29] Baroody, *Media Access,* 72-74.

[30] Williams, "Military, Media and Manipulation," D4.

[31] Pete Williams, "The Press and the Persian Gulf War," *Parameters,* XXI, no.3 (Autumn 1991), 8, http://strategicstudiesinstitute.army.mil/pubs/parameters/Articles/1991/1991%20williams.pdf (accessed October 2, 2013).

most major network executives succumbed to military demands because they saw some access and logistical support was better than no support, and they were more focused on their larger goal of sustaining their yearly $10 billion empire.[32]

As media executives looked to balance coverage and profits within the new 24/7 news cycle, several journalists claimed the Pentagon's pools and escorts limited their access and their ability to file stories, based on their requirement to sign ground rules agreements. Agreements subjected press articles to formal "security reviews" and then prevented the coverage of religious services, severely injured military personnel (until family notification), and disclosure of unit locations, but then confusingly left the decision to publish or broadcast to the reporter.[33] Although some complained about pools and escorts for justifiable reasons, others like Joe Galloway, reporting for *U.S. News and World Report,* had a different outlook. Based on Galloway's credentials and established military trust, he obtained unfettered access to the 24th Infantry Division. His ability to foster a relationship with the commanding general and to live in the field enabled him to travel, see, and learn everything General McAffrey did and saw.[34] Because of his experience and established trust, Galloway filed one of the most comprehensive stories of Desert Storm.

In addition to illuminating access challenges and the media's desire for uninhibited coverage, the Gulf War also demonstrated the media's unwavering demand for First Amendment protection. The numerous lawsuits emerging from the conflict claiming violations of the First Amendment provide tremendous insight to media goals

---

[32] Macarthur, *Second Front,* 3.
[33] Baroody, *Media Access,* 89; and Jason DeParle, "Keeping the News in Step" *New York Times,* May 6, 1991, A9, http://search.proquest.com.ezproxy6.ndu.edu/docview/108795474?accountid=12686 (accessed October 2, 2013).
[34] Baroody, *Media Access,* 132.

and the difficulties in sustaining a working relationship with the military. One of the more famous cases occurred on January 10, 1991 when the Center for Constitutional Rights filed on behalf of *Harper's, Mother Jones, The Nation, The Village Voice*, argued media pools, escorts, and security reviews violated the First Amendment.[35] Although the presiding Judge Sand, of the U.S. District Court for Southern District of New York, dismissed *The Nation Magazine, et al v. United States Department of Defense* on April 16, 1991 because the conflict ended, he raised several important issues for future coverage and the aloofness of the media. Sand explained how "the case raised new and important questions about the relationship between the First Amendment and national security, especially about the role of American journalists in wars abroad."[36] Sand also complained about the news organizations never responding to his request for more information or "providing alternatives to the Pentagon regulations that they thought would be constitutional."[37] Instead, he only received a response that the press wanted "unlimited, unilateral access."[38] Judge Sand's decision and revelation of the media's loftiness provides insight into current and future goals and desires of the press to balance constitutional rights and national security while operating in a world with advancing technologies, increased profit demands, and the inability to control access.

Although the Pentagon claimed, "mission accomplished" in their relationship with the media, the media saw the Gulf War as a failed attempt, a return to censorship. The media realized "some restrictions based on security is required but at the end of that

---

[35]Macarthur, *Second Front*, 34.

[36] Vera Haller, "Judge Dismisses Media Lawsuit Challenging Pentagon Rules," *The Associate Press,* April 16, 1991, http://www.apnewsarchive.com/1991/Judge-Dismisses-Media-Lawsuit-Challenging-Pentagon-Rules/id-d14168ebf31fabb26b3e70625d9b494e (accessed October 2, 2013).

[37] Ibid.

[38] Ibid.

conflict felt, they were working for the Pentagon and censored."[39] This polar opposite feeling emerging from the Gulf War coupled with the lessons observed from past conflicts continues to demonstrate the difficulties in the military-media relationship and sets the stage for future challenges. One continues to see the difficulty in trying to balance access and coverage with operational security and the need to communicate with stakeholders within an environment of increasing global communication. Unfortunately, the beginning of globalization and the emergence of new communication technologies like video recorders, satellites, cell and video phones, and faster Internet negated the press' requirement to request permission to access a war zone or rely on the military for logistical support. This new global order called for improved relations between the military and media, and leaders on both sides who were not only adaptive but could thrive in uncertainty and complexity.

A Decade of Operations Iraqi and Enduring Freedom

Operations in Iraq and Afghanistan serve as pinnacle examples of improved media relations. The last decade of conflict provided both the military and the media opportunities to achieve deeper understanding of one another while observing the effects of information on policy and public opinion. Throughout these operations, the media demonstrated their wavering interest, the need for profit and the relentless demand of stakeholders operating within a 24/7 information environment. Conversely, the military continued to apply lessons learned from past military-media endeavors, adapted to the powerful effects of the narrative within a globalized world, and worked to improve relations with the media.

---

[39] Baroody, *Media Access,* 123.

The OSD, Public Affairs guidance for OIF/OEF is the first illustration of this

point:

> *The (DOD) policy on media coverage of future operations is that media will*
> *have long-term, minimally restrictive access to U.S. Air, Ground, and Naval*
> *forces through embedding. Media coverage will shape public perception of*
> *the National Security environment now and in the years ahead. This holds*
> *true for the U.S. public; the public in allied countries whose opinion can*
> *affect the durability of our coalition; and publics in countries where we*
> *conduct operations, whose perceptions of us can affect the cost and duration*
> *of our involvement. Our ultimate strategic success in bringing peace and*
> *security… in our long-term commitment to supporting democratic ideals. We*
> *need to tell the factual story-good or bad-before others seed the media with*
> *disinformation and distortions…our people in the field need to tell our story-*
> *only commanders can ensure the media gets the story.[40]*

DoD clearly demonstrated their ability to learn from the past, to proactively shape the

future military-media environment rather than waiting to react to it. OSD's guidance

emphasized the need for all commanders to open their units to the media, embrace

embedding, and do a better job of keeping the American public informed.

Lieutenant General Thomas Metz illustrates the first example of a

transformational approach to harness the power of information to support operations.

While serving as Commanding General Multinational Corps-Iraq, Metz witnessed the

ability of the narrative to influence the outcome of military operations after failures in

Fallujah, April 2004. As explained in a 2006 Military Review article, Metz asserts the

operations in Fallujah failed not because of insufficient combat power but the inability to

shape the battlefield through the information domain. He continued to explain, because

of Fallujah, he and his staff created the "IO Threshold", a process enabling him to

"visualize a point which the enemy information-based operations (aimed at international,

---

[40] Office of the Secretary of Defense, *Public Affairs Guidance (PAG) on Embedding Media During Possible Future Operations/Deployments in the U.S. Central (CENTCOM) Area of Operations (AOR)*, (Wahsington D.C., 2003), 1.

regional, and local media coverage) began to undermine the Coalition forces' ability to conduct unconstrained combat operations."[41] As a result of this new adaptive approach, Metz's team postured itself to visualize and better shape the entire battlespace for subordinate commanders.

The results of better visualization coupled with an appreciation for the media's role is highlighted by the actions of then Major General Peter Chiarelli, Commanding General, 1st Cavalry Division in 2005. While preparing for the first democratic election in Iraq and reacting to an insurgent rocket attack on the "International Zone," he actively engaged the news cycle, leveraged new technology, and changed unit procedures in order to prevent a negative public opinion towards security for the upcoming election. After his soldiers filmed the attack and captured seven insurgents, Chiarelli understood the possible negative effects of these attacks on the upcoming elections so he declassified the video and proactively engaged local Iraqi media. In doing so, he and his soldiers could "calm the concerns caused by the attacks" and complete their assigned mission.[42] In addition to adapting leader and unit thinking towards information, Chiarelli and his staff were some of the first joint forces to leverage new technology -- the Digital Video and Imagery Distribution System (DVIDS) -- to transmit their narrative around the world.[43] The ability to think in terms of a 24/7 news cycle and use technology enabled Chiarelli to influence the global narrative in regards to Iraq's 2005 historic election.

---

[41] Thomas F. Metz, Mark W. Garrett, James E. Hutton, and Timothy W. Bush, "Massing Effects in the Information Domain, a Case Study in Aggressive Information Operations," *Military Review*, 86 (May-June 2006): 2-12.

[42] Peter W. Chiarelli and Patrick R. Michaelis, "Winning the Peace: The Requirement for Full-Spectrum Operations," *Military Review* 85, no. 4 (July/August 2005), 15; and *American Forces Press Service*, "Insurgents Caught After Attack on U.S. Embassy in Iraq," January 30, 2005, http://www.defense.gov/utility/printitem.aspx?print=http://www.defense.gov/news/newsarticle.aspx?id=24225 (accessed October 3, 2013).

[43] Metz, Garrett, Hutton, and Bush, *Military Review,* 11.

Similarly, to both Metz and Chiarelli, subordinate commanders also improved their appreciation of the military-media relationship and the media's ability to influence opinion. Colonel Ralph Baker (now a major general) provides the first example of a maneuver commander learning the effects of the narrative on military operations. During combat operations, Baker came to realize that the media was just as lethal as the physical destruction of the enemy. Baker, in a 2006 *Military Review* article, explained how he was not a believer in information operations but soon learned that he "could not hope to shape and set conditions for his battalions or his Soldiers to be successful" without applying aspects of information operations. Baker continued to highlight how he "had inadvertently taken for granted and failed to effectively address his own Soldiers...how his Soldiers were getting the same inaccurate, slanted news that the American public gets."[44] Additionally, he explained how "[the military] needs to ensure that information operations receive the same level of emphasis and involvement that our commanders have traditionally allocated to conventional maneuver operations."[45] Because of this change in thinking, he took measures to adapt within an environment influenced by information dissemination. In order to influence and win over the media, Baker created systems that fostered better relations with the media while enabling his subordinate commanders to focus on the friction of combat. Some such systems included unit press conferences with local media, developing weekly themes and message for his unit leaders, and changing the overall unit climate towards the media.[46]

---

[44] Ralph O. Baker, "The Decisive Weapon: A Brigade Combat Team Commander's Perspective on Information Operations," *Military Review* 86, no 3(May/June 2006), 13-15.

[45] Ibid, 31.

[46] Ibid, 19-25.

Baker's adaptive approach and ability to change the unit opinion towards media relationships demonstrates just one commander's actions to improve military-media relations. Like Baker, other commanders embraced and fostered relations with the media in order to win on the information front. For example, then Colonel and now Major General Michael Tucker demonstrated improved understanding of the narrative when he expressed "if you do not wrap your arms around the media, then you will no longer be able to influence the media…if you don't control the media, it will control you."[47] Although this paper does not advocate for controlling the media, it does advocate for the importance of allowing soldiers to tell the [military's] story, good or bad. After all, the military's story is what the American public needs to hear in order to provide reassurances their support and contributions to the military are well used.

In addition to adapting military unit procedures and culture towards media engagement, military leaders improved their media relations through gaining greater understanding of media goals. The last decade of war has allowed military leaders to adapt their media engagement strategy based on their observations and understanding of how consumer and profit demands influenced media interest. Donald Wright, the Army's Combat Studies Institute, provides an example of this trend in *On Point II*. Wright explains how during OIF after December 2004, "embeds dropped from 700 to 35 mostly likely from shifts in intensity and financial concerns of media organizations."[48] Additionally, General Daniel Allen, as a Colonel, alluded to this waning interest when he explained "the slant toward sensationalism made it hard to get them [reporters] out to cover the more routine activities…stabilization operations are a steady, often not

---

[47] Donald P. Wright and Timothy R. Reese, *On Point II: Transition to the New Campaign* (Kansas: Combat Studies Institute Press, 2008), 293.
[48] Ibid, 295-297.

glamorous, ongoing activity."[49] Regardless of the media's attention span, the military

must continue to operate under these conditions and maximize the goals of the media in

order sustain current successes in delivering the military's narrative.

In addition to adapting to the media's short attention span, military leaders

operating in OIF/OEF also learned and adapted to the media's desire for unhindered

access. While military officials believed embedding was better than no access, enabled

quicker initial coverage, served to counter false reports, and opened the doors to greater

access as fighting continued, they continued to learn that the media continued to push for

unimpeded access.[50] Conversely, Kenneth Payne explains in *Parameters* how although

embedding media "continues to provide the military control and builds stronger military-

media relationship initially, embedding also leads to a loss in the journalist's perspective

and frustration."[51] A better understanding of the media's desires for unhindered access

and unbiased reporting enables military leaders to balance operational security with

delivering their message.

The last decade of conflict tremendously contributed to the evolution of the

military's relationship with the media. The transition from the Vietnam-Era approach to

the 1980s and 1990s to the progressive attitude of current operations continues to bolster

this fragile relationship. As military leaders begin to understand and teach their

subordinates the importance of fostering a healthy discourse with the media, they will

shape the military-media relationship in a positive manner. It is imperative the joint force

continues to cooperate with its media counterparts. As the information domain expands

---

[49] Wright and Reese, *On Point II*, 297.
[50] Ibid, 294.
[51] Kenneth Payne, "The Media as an Instrument of War," *Parameters* 35, no. 1 (Spring 2005): 86-88.

and continues to evolve, so too must the military's understanding of this domain increase, including how the military and media will operate in it to each other's benefit. As such, the next chapter examines this environment and the obstacles facing both the military and the media.

CHAPTER 3: THE ENVIRONMENT

"To subdue the enemy without fighting is the acme skill. Therefore I say: Know the enemy and know yourself; in a hundred battles you will never be in peril." [1] *– Sun Tzu*

The Threat

The military faces an operational and strategic environment that is ever changing, complex, and enduring. As the Chairman of the Joint Chiefs explains in his *Capstone Concept for the Joint Operations: 2020*, "the security environment is characterized by several persistent trends: the proliferation of weapons of mass destruction, the rise of modern competitor states, violent extremism, regional instability, transnational criminal activity, and competition for resources."[2] In addition to the trends listed above, the world of information and technology continues to make this environment more complex. Further, the explosion of social media (Facebook, Twitter, Instagram, Snapchat, and others) and personal communication devices adds another layer of complexity military leaders must understand and apply to their operating environment. Because the changing nature of the enemy and how the globalization of information give "rise to a future security environment likely to be more unpredictable, complex, and potentially dangerous than today," military leaders must understand and adapt to this evolving environment.[3]

As availability of personal communication devices become more readily available, the ability to disseminate information and messages increases as do their consequences. The availability of technology provides the medium for everyone, not just

---

[1] Sun Tzu, *The Art of War,* trans., Samuel B. Griffith (New York: Oxford University Press, 1971), 77 and 84.

[2] Martin E. Dempsey, *Capstone Concept for Joint Operations: Joint Force 2020* (Washington D.C., 2012): 2, http://www.jcs.mil//content/files/2012-09/092812122654_CCJO_JF2020_FINAL.pdf (accessed October 29, 2013).

[3] Ibid, 3.

the media, to determine (regardless of values or agenda) what information the world should see. It is important to understand the speed and global effect information has on public opinion.

Two recent examples highlight the influential effects of information. The first occurred September 16, 2013, at the Navy Yard in Washington D.C. The events of the Navy Yard shooting highlight the impacts of journalist values in conflict, and even more importantly the speed of social media. Before this event surfaced on television, print, or internet news media, danger notification circulated rapidly across Facebook and Twitter. The ability of by-standers to process and then broadcast events in real-time occurred before the first news crew arrived on-scene to report the situation. This example also alludes to the powerful influence of information and the internal ethical struggle within the media. Because of journalists trying to assist law enforcement, "scoop" the story, and gain ratings, several of the first reports contained misinformation. Subsequently, *The Washington Post* and *USA Today* reported both NBC and CBS misidentified the shooter as Rollie Chance and potentially damaged his reputation as FBI and media arrived at his home to investigate the story further.[4] As illustrated by Thucydides 2500 years ago, the power of misreporting is as influential as accurate reporting in the sense most citizens take information at face value and will not explore the accuracy of reporting.

The second example of influence is the 2013 story involving Paula Deen and her testimony in a discrimination lawsuit. Due to a June 2013 *National Enquirer* story, Paula

---

[4] Tom Jackman, "Rollie Chance, Misidentified as Navy Yard Shooter, Demands Media Accountability," *The Washingotn Post*, September 20, 2013, http://www.washingtonpost.com/local/rollie-chance-misidentified-as-navy-yard-shooter-demands-media-accountability/2013/09/20/7226087e-221b-11e3-966c-9c4293c47ebe_story.html?Post+generic=%3Ftid%3Dsm_twitter_washingtonpost (accessed September 20, 2013); and Rem Rieder, "NBC, CBS Quickly Retract ID of Navy Yard Shooter," *USA Today*, September 16, 2013, http://www.usatoday.com/story/news/2013/09/16/networks-retract-id-of-dc-navy-yard-shooter/2821329/ (accessed September 20, 2013).

Deen learned firsthand the influential power of information both personally and professionally. Deen's problems began when her family fired a restaurant manager for inappropriate sexual contact with minor servers. After the Deens fired Lisa Jackson, Jackson filed a race and sex discrimination lawsuit against her former employers.[5] Because of Deen's language during her disposition and the unauthorized release of that disposition to the media, she offended both the public and her sponsors.[6] Although U.S. District Court Judge William T. Moore Jr dismissed the case because the plaintiff had no legal standing to allege discrimination based on her color, Mrs. Deen quickly saw her livelihood and reputation destroyed as society and sponsors tried and convicted her in a court of public opinion.[7] The outrage generated from this national story led sponsors to remove their support without hesitation and her character became a point of humor throughout late night television.[8] In the end, Mrs. Deen received no apologies, show of remorse, or public retraction from the plaintiff, the most outspoken critics, or her sponsors.

The above two examples highlight the influential effects of information, regardless of the medium, on public opinion. They also demonstrate the importance of the narrative and the need to insure it is accurate, as the public forms its opinion based on first reports and does little to learn all the details of a story. As Thucydides explained, "people are inclined to accept all stories…in an uncritical way – even when those stories

---

[5] Sadie Gennis, "A Timeline of Paula Deen's Downfall," *TV Guide*, http://www.tvguide.com/news/paula-deen-scandal-timeline-1067274.aspx (accessed August 25, 2013).

[6] Ibid.

[7] *AP*, "Judge OKs deal dismissing Paula Deen lawsuit," *CBSNews Online*, August 27, 2013, http://www.cbsnews.com/news/judge-oks-deal-dismissing-paula-deen-lawsuit/ (accessed February 8, 2014.)

[8] Gennis, "Paula Deen's Downfall."

concern their own native countries."[9] Military leaders are well served to heed Thucydides' words as they grapple with these environmental dynamics.

The Media

Although labeled as "the enemy" by the military, the complex "animal" called the media serves a Constitutional role within society. Military leaders need to clearly understand and appreciate that role. In so doing, military leaders will better posture themselves to transmit a timely, accurate, and transparent narrative to their constituents that is also palatable to the media. Many things affect the actions and current trends of the media. Factors such as understanding the purpose of the media, the values associated with fulfilling the media's role, and the continued development of a profession all contribute to current and potential trends of the media reporting on military affairs.

As seen through the previous chapter, the media's role evolved over time and continues to evolve in order to shape the future. The U.S. media derives its roles from the Constitution, history, and the societies it serves. Just as Siebert, et al., explained how the media reflects the political and social values of the environment it operates in, they also emphasis how history and current professional trends also define the role of the media.[10] In addition to history, technological innovation of the 20th Century and professional debates also contribute to defining the media's role. For example, the 1947 Commission on Freedom of the Press or the "Hutchins Commission Report" served such

---

[9] Thucydides, *History of the Peloponnesian War*, 46.

[10] Fred S. Siebert, Theodore Peterson, and Wilbur Schramm, *Four Theories of the Press: The Authoritarian, Libertarian, Social Responsibility, and Soviet Communist Concepts of what the Press should be and do* (Illinois: University of Illinois Press Urbana, 1978), 1.

a purpose.[11] The Hutchins Report tried to affix accountability when it called on the

American press to:

> "live up to its social responsibility and for the press to present a truthful, comprehensive account of the day's events in a context which gives meaning, serve as a forum for the exchange of comment and criticism, project a representative picture of the constituent groups of society, present and clarify the goals and values of society, and provide full access to the day's intelligence.[12]

Like the Hutchins Report, individual journalists argue and describe their role in society.

For example, journalist Rabinovitz and Jeffords argue one role of the media is to serve as

a governmental watchdog, while others describes the media's role as a "tool of checks

and balances or a Fourth Estate of government."[13] As illustrated through these examples,

the media struggles to define itself while remaining relevant to its community. The

constant struggle for internal growth and increased profit becomes more exasperated

when placed over organizational goals, the environment, and professional and personal

values and morals.

Although denigrated, journalists face the same challenges as the military

operating in today's complex global environment. Similar to the military over the last

decade of war, the media writ large struggles to redefine its role, professional ethics and

values, and relevance in society. Gallup's annual Confidence in Institution survey shows

the decline in public confidence in newspaper and television news since 1990. It shows

that no more than 25% of Americans state, "they have a great deal or quite a lot of

---

[11] Ibid, 4-5.

[12] Land, Mitchell, "Introduction," *Contemporary Media Ethics, a Practical Guide for Students, Scholars, and Professionals,* eds. Mitchell Land and Bill Hornaday (Spokane, Washington: Marquette Books, 2006), 5-9.

[13] Julianne Schultz, *Reviving the Fourth Estate: Democracy, Accountability and the Media* (United Kingdom: Cambridge University Press, 1998), 3; Lauren Rabinovitz and Susan Jeffords, "Introduction," *Seeing through the Media: The Persian Gulf War,* eds. Susan Jeffords and Lauren Rabinovitz (New Jersey: Rutgers University Press, 1994), 11.

confidence in either".[14] Additionally, the corrosion of trust supports Julianne Schultz's

plea for the media to focus on good journalism and revive the essence of the "fourth

estate." Although examining the Australian press, Schultz's argument relates to the

current struggles of U.S. journalism to balance the environment, declining public trust,

and the demands of economic pressure and stakeholder interests.[15]

As media personalities react to the decline in trust, it appears they are also

reflecting on professional values and the ability to face ethical dilemmas in delivering

information. This internal discussion of values also influences media's immediate

environment and directly affects its relationship with the military. For example,

academics like Lambeth, Land, Fuse, Lambiase, and Merrill continue the professional

debate regarding the underlying principles of the desired endstates of the media. These

scholars discuss how values affect what journalists report, what executives decide to

disseminate, and then which guiding principle – communitarian (based on society as a

whole) or utilitarian (best for the majority) – they subscribe to in order to address their

audience.[16] In discussing ethics, these scholars, especially Land, focus on the moral

values or principles of truth, humaneness, stewardship, justice and freedom, and the non-

moral (not amoral) principles of profit – the "scoop", prestige, or sweeps.[17]

---

[14] Lymari Morales, "In U.S., Confidence in Newspaper, TV News Remains a Rarity," *Gallup Politics Online*, August 13, 2010, http://www.gallup.com/poll/142133/confidence-Newspapers-news-remains-rarity.aspx. (accessed October 30, 2013).

[15] Schultz, *Reviving the Fourth Estate,* 67 and 115-116.

[16] John C. Merrill, "Contemporary Media Ethics," in *Contemporary Media Ethics, a Practical Guide for Students, Scholars, and Professionals,* eds. Mitchell Land and Bill Hornaday (Spokane, Washington: Marquette Books, 2006), 29-38; Koji Fuse, Mitchell Land, and Jacqueline J. Lambiase, "Expanding the Philosophical Base for Ethical Public Relations Practice: Cross-Cultural Case Application of Non-Western Ethical Philosophies," *Western Journal of Communication* 74, no. 4 (2010): 436-55; and Edmund Lambeth, "Elements of Media Ethics Instruction," in *Contemporary Media Ethics, a Practical Guide for Students, Scholars, and Professionals,* eds. Mitchell Land and Bill Hornaday (Spokane, Washington: Marquette Books, 2006), 57-66.

[17] Land, *Contemporary Media Ethics,* 11-15; and Mitchell Land, interviewed by author, Regent University, VA, October 9, 2013.

Just as in military service, when an individual's values (professional or personal) are in opposition they engage in an internal ethical struggle that determines thought and action. The same also holds true for journalists. For example, a major struggle contributing to today's decline in public trust revolves around profit. As Schultz explained, "global news business is overwhelming, the profits staggering, the values questionable and the power immense."[18] Macarthur, in *Second Front*, also explains how the networks earned over $10 billion in revenues in 1990.[19] Another example of profit earning is Time Warner reporting second quarter (2013) revenue growth of 10% to $7.4 billion, a quarterly record of $3.8 billion profit and an advertising growth of 11%.[20] Although earning a living is not a bad thing, the need to make a profit places journalists at odds with editors and executives of these media companies. The dilemma between holding true to providing information to the public or fighting to get the "scoop," achieve notoriety, or contributing to profit margins contributes to current struggles in the media.

In addition to profit, the conflict between non-moral and moral values -- such as notoriety and humanness or the "scoop" versus factual reporting -- continues to plague journalists and their organizations. The *Associated Press*' Malcolm Browne provides an excellent example of this type of struggle and its contribution to the opinion of the media. On June 11, 1963, while serving in Vietnam, Browne experienced a dilemma, as he had to decide between taking a politically defining picture of a monk ablaze or interfering with history and trying to save the monk.[21] Regardless of personal opinion, journalists

---

[18] Schultz, *Reviving the Fourth Estate,* 2.
[19] Macarthur, *Second Front,* 3.
[20] Corporate Communications, "Time Warner INC. Reports Second-Quarter 2013 Results," New York: One Time Warner Center, August 7, 2013, http://ir.timewarner.com/phoenix.zhtml?c=70972&p=quarterlyearnings (accessed August 10, 2013).
[21] William M. Hammond, *Reporting Vietnam: Media and Military at War* (Kansas: University Press of Kansas, 1998), 9.

must quickly resolve internal dilemmas, determine the newsworthiness of events, and then submit their work. Once completed, media executives and producers disseminate what they feel will increase profit and serve their stakeholders. The media profession is not easy and continues to adapt to today's environment, of changing societal norms and values, just as the military. It is this adaption by both institutions, which constantly contributes to the exacerbation of the delicate military-media relationship.

The Military

"We should remember we work for them [the American People]...measured and informed dialogue is their right -- and ours -- to expect and to nurture.... It is an obligation -- a requirement to explain ourselves, to justify our actions, to put into context what we are doing and why." [22] - *Rear Admiral John F. Kirby, Chief of Information*

As the military wrestles with the residual effects of a decade of continuous combat and the emerging dynamic of a resource confined environment, it is also refocusing on the fundamental nature of the military profession and the necessity of education. Not unlike the media, the military continues to struggle with values and professional behavior. As such, the rededication to the profession of arms and military values is not surprising since the Chairman focused on these same priorities in December 2010, when served as the Commanding General of the Army's Training and Doctrine Command (TRADOC).[23]

In that year, the Secretary of the Army directed Dempsey to "lead a review of the Army Profession" in order to "take a hard look at [the Army] to ensure we understand

---

[22] Mike M. Kafka, "Media Training," Naval Air Forces Atlantic (lecture, Norfolk, VA, 2013); Rear Admiral John F. Kirby, e-mail to author, November 16, 2013; and Lieutenant Commander Steven Thompson, e-mail to author, November 14, 2013.

[23] Martin E. Dempsey, "An Army White Paper: The Profession of Arms" (Fort Monroe, VA: Training and Doctrine Command. December 8, 2010), 1.

what we have been through over the past nine years, how we have changed, and how we must adapt to succeed in an era of persistent conflict."[24] This campaign to evaluate and reeducate an Army has since transcended the entire joint force. As General Dempsey moved from TRADOC to the Army's Chief of Staff and eventually to the position of the Chairman of the Joint Chiefs of Staff, his priority to the profession of arms and a values-based organization remained a priority. The importance of values and understanding what the military is and what it represents continues today, as illustrated in the 2012 publication of the *Chairman's Strategic Direction to the Joint Force*. In providing his guidance, the Chairman defines seven directives as they relate to the preservation of the profession of arms and include:

> 1) Develop and adopt lessons learned from the past decade of war. 2) Promote a culture of continuous learning and adaption at every echelon of the Joint Force. 3) Define the essential knowledge, skills, attributes, and behaviors that define the Joint Profession of Arms. 4) Institutionalize these in education, training, organizations, and policies. 5) Reinforce leadership development at all levels of Joint Professional Military Education. 6) Develop principled leaders who can combine new capabilities in new ways in complex environments. 7) Recruit and retain people with the leadership, character, and expertise needed to sustain our Profession of Arms.[25]

As amplified by five of the seven directives, it is clear that the Chairman believes education provides a solution for shaping the joint force to adapt to the future.

This call to enhance the profession of arms and prioritize both individual and intuitional education advocates for a solution and demonstrates the challenges facing the military in fostering better relationships with the media. Although marginally improving, training and education in media relations, at all levels of the force, is lacking. Consequently, this training discrepancy contributes to the

---

[24] Dempsey, "An Army White Paper," 1.
[25] Martin E. Dempsey, *Chairman's Strategic Direction to the Joint Force* (Washington DC: Joint Staff, February 6, 2012), 10.

military's lag and struggle to provide timely, accurate, and transparent narrative to its stakeholders, especially the American public.

The need to educate officers in dealing with the media is improving at higher levels but still lags at the junior officer level. As seen across both the Army and Navy, the general emphasis focuses on explaining the goals and environment of the media (especially in social media), the press' right to report, the military's obligation to inform the public, and interview procedures (including knowing your reporter and techniques for conducting an interview).[26] In addition, the time allocated to interact and foster relationships with the media ranges from on-demand to weeks. Both the Army and Navy provide examples of the growing influence of the media and the need to interact with journalists. The Navy Installation Command provides new commanders with a week of hands-on training while attending the Emergency Management Senior Leaders' Course.[27]

Comparably, in August 2013, the Army moved media training from its Tactical Commander's Development Course (focused at tactical commanders) to the all-encompassing Pre-Command Course that meets the needs of all officers slated to command at the O5/O6 level within the Army.[28] This evolution of training priority and placement speaks volumes to the increasing emphasis placed on learning how better to interact with the media and communicate the military's narrative to the public. Although both examples serve to highlight an increase in priority and understanding at the higher levels, the effect of this education is not

---

[26] Steven Thompson, e-mail to author, November 14, 2013; and Michael C. Sevcik, e-mail to author, October 24-28, 2013.

[27] Ed Buclatin, e-mail to author, November 14, 2013.

[28] Michael C. Sevcik, e-mail to author, October 24, 2013; and Michael C. Sevcik, "Communicating with the Media" (lecture, Fort Leavinworth, KS, October 24, 2013).

trickling to the lowest level -- quite possibly the most important level, as this is where the journalist focus their efforts. For example, as of date, there is no military-media training or education in the Army's pre-commissioning training, initial armor officer training, or at the Maneuver Captains Career Course (MCCC).[29]

As the military struggles with priorities and resource constraints, it is demonstrating a lag at the junior levels in trying to keep pace with the dynamic and rapidly changing information environment. In periods of declining resources, military education becomes a zero-sum game. By focusing on education, though, the joint force could improve both its relationship with the media and its narrative while enhancing the most desirable basic traits of military leaders.

---

[29] Nelson G. Kraft, e-mail to author, September 9, 2013 and the author's experience as the Professor of Military Science at George Mason University, 2009-2010, and his command of the Armor Officer Basic Leader's Course, 2010-2012.

CHAPTER 4: EDUCATION IS THE ANSWER

"Winning modern war is as much dependent on carrying the domestic and international public opinion as it is on defeating the enemy." [1] *Kenneth Payne*

"Telling the story of the United States Army and our Soldiers is not only a noble calling, but in today's information environment, it is essential to the success of our mission and to the overall success of our nation in this era of persistent conflict". [2] *Lieutenant General William B. Caldwell*

The Problem

The analysis of both the military-media relationship's history and the current information environment reflect the following enduring challenges: periods of mistrust and disdain, friction caused by legitimate but differing Constitutional objectives, a lack of organizational understanding, and periods of healthy interaction based on ad-hoc and last minutes efforts to bolster relations. As seen from the Vietnam Conflict, when strategic, operational, and public narratives differed from ground truth, military-media relationships turned mistrustful and proved to negatively influence military leaders, operations, and the military's narrative for generations. History also demonstrates the importance of trust and how once trust is lost, from both actors, it takes enormous effort and time to reestablish that trust and form productive relationships.

Additionally, this historical analysis demonstrates how differing military and media goals and their conflicting roles within U.S. society contribute to misunderstanding and strained relationships. As Kenneth Payne mentioned in his 2005, *Parameter* article, "there is always an inherent tension between the ostensible goals of impartial and balanced media reporting and the military objectives of the combatant." [3] The media will

---

[1] Kenneth Payne, "The Media as an Instrument of War," *Parameters* 35, no. 1 (Spring 2005): 81.

[2] William B. Caldwell IV, "Becoming an Effects-Based Communicator," *CALL Newsletter* no 09-11 (December 2008): 57.

[3] Payne, "Instrument of War," 84.

continue to serve as the "Fourth Estate" – or the watchdog of government, inform society, hold individuals and organizations accountable, while demanding access and earning money. Conversely, the military serves as an extension of policy, attempts to balance operational security with mission success, while striving to communicate an effective and timely message to its stakeholders. Military leaders should embrace these differences and remember the insightful comments made in 2007 by former Secretary of Defense Robert Gates when he challenged the Naval Academy graduates to:

> Remember the importance of two pillars of our freedom under the Constitution - the Congress and the press. Both surely try our patience from time to time, but they are the surest guarantees of the liberty of the American people. As officers, you will have the responsibility to communicate… to be honest and true in our reporting to them. Especially if it involves admitting mistakes or problems. The same is true with the press, in my view a critically important guarantor of our freedom. The press is not the enemy, and to treat it as such is self-defeating.[4]

Similarly, the periods of mistrust coupled with conflicting societal roles build deep-rooted biases that prevent understanding, reflection, and contribute to perpetuating negative military attitudes towards the press. By examining the modern information environment, while placing personal biases aside, both the military and the media struggle with similar issues. As globalization of information continues, both organizations contend with challenges of values, imbuing professionalism, and adaptation to a changing environment. For example, as the media contends with an increase in misreporting or journalists like *Rolling Stones*, Michael Hastings – that trade fame and profit over access and trust – the military also struggles to repair the ethical compass of senior leaders, reemphasize the profession of arms, and tries to infuse common values to a generation influenced by social media, information globalization, and entitlement.

---

[4] Robert M. Gates, *Duty* (New York: Alfred A. Knopf, 2014), 90-91.

Granted both groups collectively continue to struggle with trust, understanding, values, and a professional commitment, recent history shows a propensity to overcome these distractions and form productive relationships.

The last decade demonstrates the ability for the military to overcome its past and focus on the importance of delivering a narrative with and through the media. Military leaders are embracing President Obama's charge to "remember the lessons of history and avoid repeating the mistakes of the past when our military was left ill-prepared for the future," while overcoming their personal biases towards the media, building stronger cooperation with the media, and maximizing every opportunity found in the information domain. [5] The military must continue to maintain its trust with the American people while fostering enduring media relationships that prevent a reemergence of the "press-as-enemy syndrome." [6] In order to succeed in this endeavor, education, especially through the Joint Professional Military Education System, provides the best conduit to educate and train military leaders (over a career) on the important role of the media and their responsibility to communicate effectively.

The JPME System Provides the Means

As senior military leaders, like former Secretary Gates and the Army's Chief of Staff, General Raymond Odierno, encourage communications and relationships with both the public and the media, current levels of education throughout the five phases of Joint Professional Military Education (JPME) system do not sufficiently prioritize or address

---

[5] U.S. President, *Sustaining U.S. Global Leadership: Priorities for 21st Century Defense* (Washington DC: Government Printing Office, January 3, 2012), 1.

[6] James T. Currie, "Will the Army Ever Learn Good Media Relations Techniques? Walter Reed as a Case Study," *CALL Newsletter* no 09-11 (December 2008): 90.

such desires.[7] Although JPME spans a career through its five levels – Level 1, *Precommissioning*, Level 2, *Primary* (junior officers), Level 3, *JPME Phase I* (intermediate officers in the grade of O4 to senior officers in the grades of O5 to O6), Level 4, *JPME II* (senior officers in the grade of O5 to O6) and Level 5 *Capstone* (general and flag officers) – the current focus on media education at levels one through three is lacking.[8]

As General Dempsey articulated in his June 2013, memorandum to the joint force addressing leader attributes, education is "one of [his] top priorities in developing the Joint Force 2020."[9] Military leaders must remember this directive and not mortgage the long-term investment of education, as they adjust priorities and budgets in forging the Joint Force of 2020. The opportunities found throughout joint education are tremendous, but current media related education shortcomings found in levels one to three require a holistic look at the JPME system in order to maximize learning opportunities for all leaders – from the most junior to the most senior. Conducting this curriculum review and then carefully incorporating media related education into the JPME system provides the solution to progress – not regress – media relations, sustain and effective military narrative, and keep faith with the American people.

The current JPME system is under review, and this review offers the perfect medium which military leaders can use to provide prioritization, a common understanding, and the temporal opportunity to address current educational shortcomings.

---

[7] David Vergun, "Odierno Shares Views on Military's Relationship With Media," *Army News Service*, October 22, 2012; and U.S. Government Accountability Office, Report to Congressional Committees GAO-14-29, *Joint Military Education: Actions Needed to Implement DOD Recommendations for Enhancing Leadership Development* (Washington DC: October 2013), 7, http://www.gao.gov/assets/660/658527.pdf (accessed December 8, 2013).

[8] GAO Report 14-29, 7.

[9] Martin E. Dempsey, Memorandum, *Desired Leader Attributes for Joint Force 2020* (June 28, 2013): 1, https://jdeis.js.mil/jdeis/jel/education/cm_0166_13.pdf (accessed February 9, 2014).

For example, just as the *Capstone Concept for Joint Operation* (CCJO) used JPME to provide a "common understanding" and a "realization of mission command in joint operations," educators can apply the same logic for using JPME to incorporate and increase the importance of fostering relations with the media while communicating effectively to the public.[10]

In addition to emphasizing priority and common understanding, the current JPME system review coupled with fiscal uncertainties provide an opportune time to consider incorporating media related training – such as communication and listening skills, cultural and language awareness, leadership, and environmental awareness – throughout all levels of JPME in order to bolster military-media relationships and enable all leaders to communicate effectively. The current fiscal environment mandates the joint force to reevaluate priorities, missions, and refocus efforts in order to achieve the Joint Force 2020. The other opportunity found within JPME stems from DOD's ongoing reevaluation and implementation of the Military Education Coordination Council's (MECC) 2013 recommendations for improving joint education.[11]

In their education study findings delivered to the U.S. Government Accountability Office, the MECC explained how the joint forces are evaluating current JPME programs in order to determine "desired leader attributes as part of a career-long experience" and "any gaps in the current educational program" that produce officers capable of achieving

---

[10] Martin E. Dempsey, *Capstone Concept for Joint Operations: Joint Force 2020* (Washington D.C., 2012), 8, http://www.jcs.mil//content/files/2012-09/092812122654_CCJO_JF2020_FINAL.pdf (accessed October 29, 2013).

[11] "The Military Education Coordination Council (MECC) serves as an advisory body to the Director, Joint Staff on joint education issues, and consists of the MECC principals and a supporting working group. The MECC addressed key educational issues of interest to the joint education community, promotes cooperation and collaboration among the MECC member institutions, and coordinates joint education initiatives. The MECC principals are: DJ-7, the DDJS-ME; the presidents, commandants, and directors of the joint and Service universities and colleges; and the heads of any other JPME-accredited institutions," https://jdeis.js.mil/jdeis/index.jsp?pindex=30 (accessed February 9, 2014).

DOD's strategic vision for the Joint Force of 2020.[12] The MECC "made 21

recommendations, which collectively address the study's two objectives and span four

categories – (1) desired leader attributes, or educational outcomes; (2) joint education

continuums; (3) lifelong learning and advancements in learning technologies; and (4)

faculty quality."[13] The MECC's recommendations, fiscal austerity, and the strategic

shifting of effort within national instruments of power, create an ideal time to not only

incorporate media-related education throughout all levels of JPME, but also achieves

senior leaders desires effectively telling the military's story.

The Proposed Education and Training Plan

The proposed media-related education and training should not burden

current programs but enhance them. This training is not a fad and is more

than just PowerPoint® and mandatory annual training. With minor

adjustments to current curriculums, military leaders can incorporate media

education throughout all five levels of JPME, especially within levels one to

three – junior leaders. The author proposes the following education and

training guidelines:

1) Greater focus on interpersonal skills – leading, building trust, and communicating (talking and listening)
2) Continue to emphasize and incentivize foreign language training during accessions
3) Integrate cultural awareness and language training throughout all training and education – JPME phases one through five
4) Increase the importance of information operations and communication in military doctrine
5) Increase media understanding and physical media interaction for all service members.[14]

---

[12] GAO Report 14-29, Highlights section.

[13] Ibid, 32.

[14] Recommended training stems from the author's observations and is influenced by readings from Major General Baker, "The Deceive Weapon," and Dennis M. Murphy, Director of the Information

This education not only improves military-media relationships and dissemination of an effective narrative it enables greater understanding of the environment, while simultaneously improving individual military leaders and assisting units with gaining proficiency in their mission essential tasks (METL). Additionally, these recommendations produce leaders that imbue the CJCS's desired leader attributes to:

> (1) understand the environment and the effect of all instruments of national power, (2) anticipate and adapt to surprise and uncertainty, (3) recognize change and lead transitions, (4) operate on intent through trust, empowerment, and understanding (Mission Command), (5) make ethical decisions based on the shared values of the Profession of Arms, and (6) think critically and strategically in applying joint warfighting principles and concepts to joint operations.[15]

Simultaneously, the proposed training contributes to achieving seven of the 21 MECC's recommendations to:

- Develop/refine appropriate educational outcomes across a career.
- Review specific subject areas for increased emphasis within joint education on cyber warfare, cultural considerations in planning, interagency and intergovernmental operations, information and economic instruments of national power, writing with precision, operations with private entities, and professional ethics.
- The joint training community should conduct/continue efforts aimed at achieving the desired leader attributes.
- Joint functional communities should incorporate the desired leader attributes into their education and training programs as appropriate.
- Strengthen the educational outcomes at the primary level of joint education for junior officers while retaining balance with service primary level educational requirements.
- Explore potential opportunities for making increased joint education content available for junior officers via distance learning capabilities.
- Services should explore opportunities to incentivize and reward lifelong learning.[16]

Warfare Group at the US Army War College, "In Search of the Art and Science of Strategic Communication," *Parameters* 39, no. 4 (Winter 2009-10): 105-116.

[15] Dempsey, *Desired Leader Attributes*, 1; and GAO Report 14-29, 13.

[16] GAO Report 14-29, 32-33.

Although some military services have improved media and information environment education at senior officer levels – JPME levels four and five – much improvement is required at JPME levels one through three. Beginning at level one and emphasized throughout level three, military leaders need to constantly build and strengthen their interpersonal skills. These bedrock skills – developing trust, effectively communicating (writing and listening), building teams and character – enable military leaders to improve their relations with media personalities, enhance their ability to effectively communicate, and influence others.[17] The key traits of leading, as described throughout *ADP 6-22* and *ADRP 6-22* (leads, communicates, influences, and trusts) are critical in developing the overall attributes of junior leaders and indirectly contribute to fostering better media relationships and producing an effective narrative. By enhancing these traits, military leaders can learn to apply these same traits to building enduring and trusting relationships, communicate and "extend their influence beyond the chain of command," listen actively, and appreciate the ability to empathize with others.[18]

While the skills mentioned above seem common practice in military leaders, some highlight that these same skills – especially trust – contribute to fostering better media relationships. For example, in their description of the military-media relationship as a "dysfunctional marriage," both Lieutenant

---

[17] U.S. Army, Army Doctrine Publication, *Army Leadership*, ADP 6-22 (Washington DC: Army Chief of Staff, September 10, 2012), 5-8; and U.S. Army, Army Doctrine Reference Publication, *Army Leadership*, ADRP 6-22 (Washington DC: Army Chief of Staff, August 1, 2012), 6-1-6-14.
[18] *ADRP 6-22*, 6:6-14.

General Mark Hertling and Thom Shanker define one of the hardest but most important skills required by both the military and the media is trust.[19] Likewise, retired Colonel Steven Boylan, former senior PAO to General Petraeus, explains in *Military Review* how the military-media relationship is "an exercise in strategic patience" and how "developing trusting relationships, knowing [your] reporter and preparing for the media" best serve military leaders.[20] Consequently, military leaders do not need to lose the trust and confidence – as seen in the Vietnam Conflict – of the media or the public again. As a result, it is important to utilize the same interpersonal skills required by military leaders to command their units to stress the importance and time required to bolster relationships with the media and the public.

The second and third ways to enhance the military narrative and improve understanding is for military leaders to receive more directed and self-paced language and culture training. Again, focusing on JPME level one, military programs – such as Reserve Officer Training Corps programs – should not only continue requiring but also incentivize language training in pre-commissioning programs. Additionally, developing this expectation early and then requiring language development over a career enables the joint force to produce leaders that are more apt to understand culture long-term and communicate more effectively instead of receiving a "crash" course prior to deploying. Similarly, other language and cultural opportunities – such as

---

[19] Thom Shanker and Mark Hertling, "The Military-Media Relationship, A Dysfunctional Marriage?" *Military Review* 89, no 5 (September/October 2009), 2-9; and Steven A. Boylan, "The Military-Media Relationship, an Exercise in Strategic Patience," *Military Review* 91, no 5 (September/October 2011), 2-11.
[20] Boylan, "The Military-Media Relationship," 4-10.

Rosetta Stone ® – should be reintroduced, funded, and mandated throughout a military career. Because language and culture understanding contribute to desired leader attributes, better military-media relationships, and more effective narratives, the joint force should fund these opportunities and then link language and cultural gates to military education and advancement. The ability to adjust educational requirements based on a leader's cultural needs empowers that leader to improve both personally, professionally, and at his own pace. Additionally, cultural and language training enables a military leader to communicate effectively by delivering the right message, to the right audience, and at the right time. For example, in the 1860s, the U.S. Army's and settlers' lack of understanding the importance of the buffalo or "animal spirits" to the Plain Indians exacerbated deteriorating relations and contributed to armed hostilities between the Indians and the U.S. government.[21] This example highlights the importance of understanding culture, languages, and the devastating effects on influence when they are absent.

In the same way cultural and language skills contribute to greater understanding of the environment, a greater emphasis on the effects of the information domain in military doctrine and training – throughout all JPME levels – will improve media relations and the military narrative. As General Baker espoused in 2006, "we [the military] need to ensure that information operations receive the same level of emphasis and involvement that our commanders have traditionally allocated to conventional maneuver

---

[21] Bob Drury and Tom Clavin, *The Heart of Everything That Is* (New York: Simon & Schuster, 2013) 183-4.

operations."[22] This emphasis on information operations needs to carry over to both media interaction and improving understanding of the effects of information on all military endeavors. Understanding the environment not only needs touch every level of JPME, this understanding should reach every service member. In light of current events, all service members need to understand the potential impacts of their individual actions on themselves personally, the public perception of the joint force, overall mission accomplishment, and the strategic environment (e.g., reflection on U.S. policy). For instance, if Marines or Soldiers understood the information environment better and the potential effects of their actions on military missions, they may not have urinated on enemy combatants, posed inappropriately with a flag draped coffin, or hid from saluting the American flag during Retreat.[23] Although there are probably other factors contributing to these actions, a greater understanding of the environment may improve decision-making and actions – based on professional ethics and values – while sustaining the positive image of the U.S. military.

The final training recommendation includes integrating media interaction in all training events and focuses different outcomes across

[22] Baker, "The Decisive Weapon," 31.

[23] Cheryl K. Chumley, "Marine Sergeant Demoted for Urinating on Dead Taliban Militant," *The Washington Times*, August 8, 2013, http://m.washingtontimes.com/news/2013/aug/8/marine-sergeant-demoted-urinating-dead-taliban-mil/ (accessed March 12, 2014); Jon Harper, "National Guard Soldier Suspended Over 'Distasteful' Military Funeral Photos and Comments," *Stars and Stripes*, February 18, 2014, http://www.stripes.com/news/us/national-guard-soldier-suspended-over-distasteful-military-funeral-photos-and-comments-1.268422 (accessed March 12, 2014); and Douglas Ernst, " Soldier Hides to Avoid Saluting Flag, Brags About it on Instagram," *The Washington Times*, February 25, 2014, http://m.washingtontimes.com/news/2014/feb/25/soldier-hides-avoid-saluting-flag-brags-about-it-i/ (accessed March 12, 2014).

different levels of JPME. Incorporating more media engagements within all military training serves to condition younger leaders to interact with journalists confidently while assisting those leaders with understanding the pitfalls of the information environment, developing enduring media relationships, and communicating honestly with the public. Greater media interaction at the intermediate officer level (O4-O5) not only begins to condition those officers on the importance of information operations during all military missions, but also enables them to establish or strengthen their media and public relationships. Finally, this increased integration – especially by (O5-O6) level commanders – stresses the importance of media education and contributes to developing generations of leaders infused with a greater appreciation of the information environment, the importance of fostering relationships with the media, the media's potential, and the need and effect of the military's story.

The main goal of this education, that spans all five phases of JPME, is to infuse a joint force capable of thriving long-term in a complex and rapidly evolving operating environment influenced by multiple narratives. Military leaders must overcome their begrudging biases towards the media and learn to thrive in the uncertain, fast paced, and complex information domain. They must operate confidently within this domain or suffer the possible devastating consequence of avoiding it. Just as Thom Shanker explained, "I can't guarantee your story will be told the way you want it. But if you don't speak with reporters, I can guarantee your side of the story may not be told at all. Or it may be told by others who spend little time trying to understand what you do and cannot appreciate your interests at all."[24]

Another goal of this education is to enhance current programs while not burdening military commanders with mandatory and separate tasks that contribute to filling "white space" on a training calendar. This education and training should complement scheduled unit training, as well as, enhance self-study programs. Although the proposed education to 1) provide greater focus on interpersonal skills, 2) continue to emphasize and provide incentives for foreign skills during accessions, 3) integrate cultural awareness training in all training, 4) increase the importance of information operations and communication in military doctrine, and 5) increase media training provided to all servicemen, contributes to creating the Joint Force 2020, these recommendations must overcome at least two challenges.

Today's Challenges

Today's major challenges are two fold – the first challenge is to achieve service buy-in to the proposed recommendations, and the second is to balance, not mortgage, education in favor of readiness and fiscal uncertainty. First, these recommendations require each military service to accept their usefulness in sustaining both leader development and readiness. These recommendations are achievable with only minor adjustments to current JPME programs, and can enhance current efforts while enhancing already scheduled training. For example and as highlighted in chapter three, the Army and Navy are already expanding their media education and training for senior officers – commanders, executive officers, and flag officers. The proposed training advocates for

---

[24] Shanker and Hertling, "The Military-Media Relationship," 8.

expanding on such Army and Navy efforts and then distributing those educational opportunities to the lowest level.

The second challenge is for the military to prevent maintaining readiness at the expense of education and leader development. Military leaders must focus on long-term objectives, balance priorities, and commit to innovative solutions that not only contribute to leader development but also postures the Joint Force 2020 to face the future. The joint force is well served to follow historical examples of leaders like Pershing, Patton, and Marshall after World War I, or like DePuy and Starry after Vietnam. These leaders saw the effects of limited thinking and went out to reshape the Army and the military equally.[25] Just as General Pershing reflected on WWI and selected bright and rising leaders to advance military doctrine, current military leaders can do the same and select successful leaders to advance education in fiscal uncertainty.[26] At great risk to personal careers, generals like Patton, Eisenhower, and Marshall advanced the joint force by charismatically prioritizing and stressing education in the face of tremendous fiscal and political uncertainty.

Likewise, generals DePuy and Starry used education and innovative thinking to rise the hollowed 1970's Army from despair to an Army capable of dominating in future conflicts. As the Continental Army Command (CONRAC) reorganized into Forces Command (FORSCOM) and Training and Doctrine Command (TRADOC), DePuy and Starry improved equipment modernization, as well as, created the Army Training and Evaluation Program (ATREP) that educated, certified, and prepared several generations

[25] Patrick Wright, *Tank* (New York: Viking, 2000), 193-196; Mark A. Stoler, *George C. Marshall, Soldier-Statesman of the American Century* (New York: Simon & Schuster, 1989), 41-49; and Richard M. Swain, "Airland Battle," In *Camp Colt to Desert Storm, The History of U.S. Armored Forces*, eds. George F. Hoffmann and Donn A. Starry (Kentucky: The University Press of Kentucky, 1999), 360-402.

[26] Wright, *Tank,* 193-196; and Stoler, *Marshall*, 41-42.

of military leaders to face the complexity of warfare.[27] Similar to Patton and Marshall, General Starry broke traditional career paths and went out to "get the Army off its ass" and improve training and education.[28]

The proposed training, with minor adjustment to current JPME programs and unit training, should complement those endeavors and only cost commanders a small amount of additional planning time – reaching out and integrating media into already planned training events – and the time of local journalists – who are always looking for possible stories. As the author learned by serving in the Army's Cadet Command and Training and Doctrine Command, readiness, training, and education are all zero-sum endeavors. Regardless of this fact, joint force leaders – especially commanders – can contribute to developing the desired leader attributes, improving military-media relations, and delivering a powerful narrative to the public, by completing the review of the JPME system and then proactively implementing the five media education recommendations proposed in this paper. By leveraging the JPME system to improve interpersonal skills, expand cultural and language understanding, increase the focus of media training and information operations within service and joint doctrine, and increase media engagement for service members, military leaders will not only produce agile and adaptive leaders ready to advance the Joint Force 2020, but also, they will strengthen media relationships and produce an effective narrative that clearly tells the military's story and garners trust and support.

---

[27] Swain, "Airland Battle," 362-365.
[28] Ibid, 368.

CHAPTER 5: CONCLUSION

...effective strategic communications are essential to sustaining global legitimacy and supporting our policy aims. Aligning our actions with our words is a shared responsibility that must be fostered by a culture of communication throughout government. We must also be more effective in our deliberate communication and engagement and do a better job understanding the attitudes, opinions, grievances, and concerns of peoples...Doing so allows us to convey credible, consistent messages and to develop effective plans, while better understanding how our actions will be perceived. We must also use a broad range of methods for communicating with foreign publics, including new media.[1] President Barack Obama

Military leaders who can adapt to the new dynamic operating environment, consider historical lessons, and harness the opportunities offered by the Joint Professional Military Education (JPME) system can advance current successful military-media relationships while maximizing the effectiveness of the military's message to stakeholders. First, the evolving information environment will continue to have a profound influence over all military operations. As "the widespread diffusion of telecommunications technologies and digital media changes the relationship between the governed and their governments," those that understand the information environment are more apt to shape public support for their objectives.[2] Because of this "democratization" of media (the ability of just about every person on earth to find a voice), the ability of information to influence public opinion and national strategy, and the inability to control information, military leaders ignore and marginalize operating in the information

---

[1] U.S. President, *National Security Strategy,* Washington DC: Government Printing Office, May 2010, 16.

[2] Martin E. Dempsey, "The Future of Joint Operations, Real Cooperation for Real Threats," *Foreign Affairs,* (June 2013):1.

domain at their own peril.[3] Finally, the growing gap of understanding between

the American public and their military further exacerbates the complexity of the

operating environment and creates the demand to deliver an effective narrative

that informs and tells the military's story.

Cohn and Funk highlight this growing gap in a PEWS study and continue

to highlight "how only one-half of one percent of Americans serve their

country."[4] Similarly, Major General Batschelet, commander, U.S. Army's

Recruiting Command, described challenges in recruiting caused by this gap or

"social rift… and how society publicly applauds its soldiers, but is not connected

with, able to fund, or willing to provide real support to its Army."[5] This

separation between society and the military is important to understand when

trying to communicate an effective message and sustain support. If only less than

one percent people serve, the remaining population – upwards of 90 and 95% –

have only a macro understanding of what the military does. Therefore, the need

for an accurate, timely, and transparent message to the America people becomes

more crucial as the gap of understanding between the military and public grows.

In order to meet the demands created by the environment, military leaders must

continue to use historical lessons and education to foster healthy media

relationships and enable them to effectively communicate with the public,

Congress, and world.

---

[3] Colonel (retired) Peter Mansoor, PhD, History professor at The Ohio State and former exeuctive officer to General Petraeus, e-mail to author on January 3, 2014.

[4] D'vera Cohn and Cary Funk, "The Public and the Military," in *The Military-Civilian Gap, War and Sacrifice in the Post-9/11 Era,* ed. Paul Taylor, PEW Social and Demographic Trends, Pew Research Center (Washington DC, October 5, 2011), 66.

[5] Allen Batschelet, Rick Ayer, and Mike Runey, "The Army We Need; The Army We Can Have," *ARMY* 64, no 2 (February 2014), 30-32.

With the explosion of social media and communication technologies, the days of controlled access and censorship are over. Therefore, military leaders may assume the public possesses a broad understanding of the military's purpose, and must "guard against selling a narrative that is politically enticing but sell one that is realistic."[6] In order to produce this message, a military leader must reflect on history, set aside personal biases, and work across all media forms – Facebook, Instagram, Twitter, etc. – in order to influence and reach his audiences. History is important as it shows an enduring struggle between the military and the media executing their constitutionally directed roles. It also shows that journalists often received undue criticism and blame because of the military's lack of understanding or ability to accept the media's social responsibility. Although the media is not the enemy, the guidance provided by Sun Tzu remains prophetic – to understand not only wins on the conventional battlefield but also the battle of the narrative. The Joint Force 2020 can achieve this greater understanding through a focused and experiential educational approach.

As NBC Pentagon correspondent, Jim Miklaszewski, explained how current military-media relations are "the best military-media relationships in 30 years," military leaders could use the JPME system to not only develop leaders that imbue desirable leader attributes, but also to educate the force on how to advance media relationships and deliver an effective narrative.[7] Exploiting the opportunities presented in current fiscal uncertainty and the call to examine joint education objectives, enables military leaders to incorporate media-related education and training across all phases of JPME – especially

---

[6] Richard Hart Sinnreich, "An Army for Short Wars Is the Wrong Narrative," *ARMY* 64, no 2, February 2014, 16-17.
[7] Courtney Kube, NBC Pentagon National Security Producer, e-mail to author, January 30, 2014.

during the first two phases focused on junior leaders. While the influential power of the narrative continues to expands services must not only educate and train senior leaders but also must educate their junior leaders to excel at the tip of the "information spear" and carry an effective message to the public.[8] The advances made by both the Army and the Navy in providing media focused training to their senior commanders and officers can serve as an example across the military; but, these advances must also trickle down throughout the entire joint force. Therefore, as the responsibility of delivering the military's message to America falls on all service members, the joint force can use the five phases of the JPME structure to provide the proper prioritization and standardization for advancing current successful media relations and delivering a timely, accurate, and transparent narrative that inform multiple audiences.

The five recommendations provided carefully consider current fiscal limitations and the zero-sum dilemma of balancing education with readiness. Additionally, these recommendations will advance media relationships and the military's narrative while developing required leader attributes and cultural skills. Education is not only critical in developing leaders, but also provides the ways required by military leaders to defeat uncertainty and posture the Joint Force 2020 for success in future conflicts.

---

[8] Paul Taylor, ed., *The Military-Civilian Gap, War and Sacrifice in the Post-9/11 Era*, PEW Social and Demographic Trends, Pew Research Center (Washington DC, October 5, 2011), 60-68.

BIBLIOGRAPHY

Adler, Margot. "The Vietnam War, Through Eddie Adams' Lens." in *NPR.org*. March 24, 2009. http://www.npr.org/templates/transcript/transcript.php?storyId=102112403 (accessed November 19, 2013).

American Forces Press Service. "Insurgents Caught After Attack on U.S. Embassy in Iraq." Washington, DC, January 30, 2005. http://www.defense.gov/utility/printitem.aspx?print=http://www.defense.gov/news/newsarticle.aspx?id=24225 (accessed October 3, 2013).

Associated Press, 50th Anniversary. "The Burning Monk: A Defining Moment Photographed by *AP*'s Malcolm Browne," June 2013. http://www.ap.org/explore/the-burning-monk/ (accessed November 19, 2013).

Baker, Ralph O. "The Decisive Weapon: A Brigade Combat Team Commander's Perspective on Information Operations." *Military Review* 86, no. 3 (May/June 2006), 13-32. http://web.ebscohost.com.ezproxy6.ndu.edu/ehost/pdfviewer/pdfviewer?sid=d1a74f93-aa4a-4d42-8354-5c5b43341c6c%40sessionmgr114&vid=5&hid=125 (accessed August 15, 2013).

Bagdikian, Ben H. "Forward" in John R. Macarthur, *Second Front, Censorship and Propaganda in the Gulf War*. California: University of California Press, 1992.

Baroody, Judith Raine. *Media Access and the Military: The Case of the Gulf War*. Maryland: University Press of America, 1998.

Batschelet, Allen, Rick Ayer, and Mike Runey. "The Army We Need; The Army We Can Have." *ARMY* 64, no. 2 (February 2014): 30-32.

Boylan, Steven A. "The Military-Media Relationship, an Exercise in Strategic Patience." *Military Review* 91, no. 5 (September/October 2011): 2-11.

Braestrup, Peter. *Big Story: How the American Press and Television Reported and Interpreted the Crisis of Tet 1968 in Vietnam and Washington*. Colorado: Westview Press, 1977.

Caldwell, William B., IV. "Becoming an Effects-Based Communicator," *CALL Newsletter* no. 09-11 (December 2008): 57-62.

Cecil, Kelly, and Mark Sullivan. *Media War Coverage and Pentagon Policy, Policy Analysis Exercise,* submitted to the Honorable J. Daniel Howard, Assistant Secretary of Defense (Public Policy), Massachusetts: Harvard University, 1989. http://www.dod.mil/pubs/foi/administration_and_Management/other/379.pdf (accessed October 2, 2013).

Chiarelli, Peter W., and Patrick R. Michaelis. "Winning the Peace: The Requirement for Full-Spectrum Operations." *Military Review* 85, no. 4 (July/August 2005): 4-17.

Cohn, D'vera and Cary Funk. "The Public and the Military," in *The Military-Civilian Gap, War and Sacrifice in the Post-9/11 Era.* Edited by Paul Taylor. PEW Social and Demographic Trends. Pew Research Center (Washington DC, October 5, 2011): 59-72. http://www.pewsocialtrends.org/files/2011/10/veterans-report.pdf (accessed September 9, 2013).

Corporate Communications. *Time Warner INC. Reports Second-Quarter 2013 Results*, New York: One Time Warner Center, August 7, 2013. http://ir.timewarner.com/phoenix.zhtml?c=70972&p=quarterlyearnings. (accessed August 10, 2013).

Crane, Gregory R. Editor. Perseus Digital Library. "The Political Uprising at the North." *The Daily Dispatch*. http://www.perseus.tufts.edu/hopper/text;jsessionid=0D9E6086D76B9E7017C3D5E2650622E5?doc=Perseus%3atext%3a2006.05.0578. (accessed September 9, 2013).

Currie, James T. "Will the Army Ever Learn Good Media Relations Techniques? Walter Reed as a Case Study." *CALL Newsletter* no. 09-11 (December 2008): 85-93.

Dempsey, Martin E. "An Army White Paper: The Profession of Arms." Fort Monroe, VA: Training and Doctrine Command, December 8, 2010.

Dempsey, Martin E. *Chairman's Strategic Direction to the Joint Force.* Washington DC: Joint Staff, February 6, 2012.

Dempsey, Martin E. *Capstone Concept for Joint Operations: Joint Force 2020.* Washington D.C., 2012. http://www.jcs.mil//content/files/2012-09/092812122654_CCJO_JF2020_FINAL.pdf (accessed October 29, 2013).

Dempsey, Martin E. "The Future of Joint Operations, Real Cooperation for Real Threats." *Foreign Affairs* (June 2013):1. http://www.foreignaffairs.com/articles/139524/martin-e-dempsey/the-future-of-joint-operations (accessed 3 September 2013).

Dempsey, Martin E. Memorandum. *Desired Leader Attributes for Joint Force 2020* (June 28, 2013): 1-2. https://jdeis.js.mil/jdeis/jel/education/cm_0166_13.pdf (accessed February 9, 2014).

DeParle, Jason, Special to the *New York Times*. "Keeping the News in Step: Are the Pentagon's Gulf War Rules here to Stay?" *New York Times*. May 6, 1991, 1991. A9. http://search.proquest.com.ezproxy6.ndu.edu/docview/108795474?accountid=12686. (accessed October 2, 2013).

Drury, Bob and Tom Clavin. *The Heart of Everything That Is*. New York: Simon & Schuster, 2013.

Fuse, Koji, Mitchell Land, and Jacqueline J. Lambiase. "Expanding the Philosophical Base for Ethical Public Relations Practice: Cross-Cultural Case Application of Non-Western Ethical Philosophies." *Western Journal of Communication* 74, no. 4 (2010): 436-55.

Gallagher, Gary W. "The Net Result of the Campaign Was in Our Favor: Confederate Reaction to the Maryland Campaign, " in *The Antietam Campaign*. Edited by Gary W. Gallagher. North Carolina: University of North Carolina Press, 1999.

Gates, Robert M. *Duty*. New York: Alfred A. Knopf, 2014.

Haller, Vera. "Judge Dismisses Media Lawsuit Challenging Pentagon Rules," *The Associate Press*. April 16, 1991. http://www.apnewsarchive.com/1991/Judge-Dismisses-Media-Lawsuit-Challenging-Pentagon-Rules/id-d14168ebf31fabb26b3e70625d9b494e. (accessed October 2, 2013).

Hallin, Daniel C. "The Media, the War in Vietnam, and Political Support: A Critique of the Thesis of an Oppositional Media." *Journal of Politics* 46:1 (February 1984): 2-, no. 1 (02, 1984): 2-24. http://ezproxy6.ndu.edu/login?url=http://search.ebscohost.com/login.aspx?direct=true&db=aph&AN=4810766&site=ehost-live&scope=site (accessed September 22, 2013).

Hammond, William M. *Reporting Vietnam: Media and Military at War*. Kansas: University Press of Kansas, 1998.

Jeffords, Susan and Lauren Rabinovitz. eds. *Seeing through the Media: The Persian Gulf War*. New Jersey: Rutgers University Press, 1994.

Lambeth, Edmund. "Elements of Media Ethics Instruction," in *Contemporary Media Ethics, a Practical Guide for Students, Scholars, and Professionals*. Edited by Mitchell Land and Bill Hornaday. Spokane, Washington: Marquette Books, 2006.

Land, Mitchell and Bill Hornaday. eds. *Contemporary Media Ethics, a Practical Guide for Students, Scholars, and Professionals*. Spokane, Washington: Marquette Books, 2006.

Land, Mitchell. "Introduction," in *Contemporary Media Ethics, A Practical Guide for Students, Scholars, and Professionals*. Edited by Mitchell Land and Bill Hornaday. Spokane, Washington: Marquette Books, 2006.

Macarthur, John R. *Second Front, Censorship and Propaganda in the Gulf War*. California: University of California Press, 1992.

Mohrs, Charles. "Street Clashes go on in Vietnam, Foe Still Holds Parts of the Cities," *New York Times*, February 2, 1968. 1. http://search.proquest.com.ezproxy6.ndu.edu/docview/118305054/pageviewPDF?accountid=12686. (accessed November 19, 2013).

McLane, Brendan R. "Reporting from the Sandstorm: An Appraisal of Embedding." *Parameters* 34, no. 1 (Spring 2004): 77-88. http://search.proquest.com.ezproxy6.ndu.edu/military/docview/198042048/13FF43DE67737DA8F70/9?accountid=12686 (accessed August 17, 2013).

Merrill, John C. "Contemporary Media Ethics." in *Contemporary Media Ethics, A Practical Guide for Students, Scholars, and Professionals.* Edited by Mitchell Land and Bill Hornaday. Spokane, Washington: Marquette Books, 2006.

Metz, Thomas F., Mark W. Garrett, James E. Hutton, and Timothy W. Bush. "Massing Effects in the Information Domain, a Case Study in Aggressive Information Operations." *Military Review* 86 (May-June 2006): 2-12.

McGinn, Dennis and William French. "Basic Media Training." In-briefing presentation for the Washington Navy Yard Recovery. E-mail to author, November 8, 2013.

Morales, Lymari. "In U.S., Confidence in Newspaper, TV News Remains a Rarity," in Gallup Politics Online, August 13, 2010. http://www.gallup.com/poll/142133/confidence-Newspapers-news-remains-rarity.aspx (accessed October 30, 2013).

Murphy, Dennis M. "In Search of the Art and Science of Strategic Communication." *Parameters* 39, no. 4 (Winter 2009-10): 105-116. (accessed February 12, 2014).

Murphy, Dennis M. "The Future of Influence in Warfare." *Joint Force Quarterly* 64, no. 1 (October-December 2012): 47-51.

New York Times. "Military Criticisms of the Newspaper Press." *New York Times,* November 12, 1861. http://search.proquest.com.ezproxy6.ndu.edu/docview/91619648/14073AA2F267354B343/1?accountid=12686. (accessed September 11, 2013).

Office of Secretary of Defense. *"Public Affairs Guidance on Embedding Media During Possible Future Operations/Deployment in the US Central Command's (CENTCOM) Area of Responsibility (AOR)."* February 10, 2003. http://www.defense.gov/news/feb2003/d20030228pag.pdf. (accessed 3 Oct 2013).

Payne, Kenneth. "The Media as an Instrument of War." *Parameters* 35, no. 1 (Spring 2005): 81-93.

Pfau, Michael, Michel M. Haigh, Lindsay Logsdon, Christopher Perrine, James P. Baldwin, Rick E. Breitenfeldt, Joel Cesar, Dawn Dearden, Greg Kuntz, Edgar Montalvo, Dwaine Roberts, and Richard Romero. "Embedded Reporting during the Invasion and Occupation of Iraq: How the Embedding of Journalists Affects Television News Reports." *Journal of Broadcasting & Electronic Media* 49, no. 4 (2005): 468-87. http://ezproxy6.ndu.edu/login?url=http://search.ebscohost.com/login.aspx?direct=true&db=aph&AN=19432857&site=ehost-live&scope=site. (accessed August 17, 2013).

Rabinovitz, Lauren and Susan Jeffords. "Introduction," in *Seeing through the Media: The Persian Gulf War*. Edited by Susan Jeffords and Lauren Rabinovitz. New Jersey: Rutgers University Press, 1994.

Rumsfeld, Donald H. Speech Delivered to Council on Foreign Relations. New York: February 17, 2006. http://www.defense.gov/speeches/speech.aspx?speechid=27. (accessed Oct 3, 2013).

Sarantakes, Nicholas E., ed. *The Okinawa Battle Diaries of Simon Bolivar Buckner, Jr. and Joseph Stilwell, Seven Stars*, Texas: Texas A& M University Press, 2004.

Schultz, Julianne. *Reviving the Fourth Estate: Democracy, Accountability and the Media*. United Kingdom: Cambridge University Press, 1998.

Sharkey, Jacqueline. "Prime-Time Pete." *The Washington Post*, May 2, 1993. C2, http://search.proquest.com.ezproxy6.ndu.edu/docview/140896483?accountid=12686. (accessed October 2013)

Shanker, Thom and Mark Hertling. "The Military-Media Relationship, A Dysfunctional Marriage?" *Military Review* 89, no 5 (September/October 2009), 2-9.

Sheehan, Neil. *A Bright Shining Lie, John Paul Vann and America in Vietnam*. New York: Random House, 1988.

Siebert, Fred S., Theodore Peterson, and Wilbur Schramm. *Four Theories of the Press: The Authoritarian, Libertarian, Social Responsibility, and Soviet Communist Concepts of what the Press should be and do*. Illinois: University of Illinois Press Urbana, 1978.

Simpson, Brooks D. "General McClellan's Bodyguard, the Army of the Potomac after Antietam," in The Antietam Campaign. Edited by Gary W. Gallagher. North Carolina: The University of North Carolina Press, 1999.

Sinnreich, Richard Hart. "An Army for Short Wars Is the Wrong Narrative." *ARMY* 64, no. 2, (February 2014): 16-17.

Stoler, Mark A. *George C. Marshall, Soldier-Statesman of the American Century.* New York: Simon & Schuster, 1989.

Summers, Tony. "Visual Information's Impact on Battlefield Visualization." *Army Communicator* 21, no. 2 (Spring 1996): 15-16.

Sun Tzu. *The Art of War.* Translated by Samuel B. Griffith. New York: Oxford University Press, 1971.

Swain, Richard M. "Airland Battle," in *Camp Colt to Desert Storm, the History of U.S. Armored Forces.* Edited by George F. Hoffmann and Donn A. Starry. Kentucky: The University Press of Kentucky, 1999.

Sylvester, Judith L. and Suzanne Huffman. *Reporting from the Front: The Media and the Military.* Maryland: Rowman & Littlefield, 2005.

Taylor, Paul, ed. *The Military-Civilian Gap, War and Sacrifice in the Post-9/11 Era.* PEW Social and Demographic Trends. Pew Research Center. Washington DC: October 5, 2011. http://www.pewsocialtrends.org/files/2011/10/veterans-report.pdf. (accessed September 9, 2013).

Thucydides. *History of the Peloponnesian War*, Translated by Rex Warner, New York: Penguin Group, 1972.

The Civil War Trust. "Alexander Gerner." http://www.civilwar.org/education/history/biographies/alexander-gardner.html. (accessed September 11, 2013).

The Daily Dispatch. "McClellan's Great Victory-Now Forward to Richmond." Richmond. http://chroniclingamerica.loc.gov/lccn/sn84024738/1862-09-23/ed-1/seq-1/. (accessed September 9, 2013).

The Daily Dispatch. "Rebellion Crushed." Richmond. http://chroniclingamerica.loc.gov/lccn/sn84024738/1862-09-23/ed-1/seq-2/. (accessed September 9, 2013)

The Mercury. "The Defensive Policy." *The Charleston Mercury*, September 30, 1862.

The Richmond Daily Dispatch. "The Political Uprising at the North." September 23, 1862. Richmond. http://chroniclingamerica.loc.gov/lccn/sn84024738/1862-09-23/ed-1/seq-1/#date1=09%2F23%2F1862&index=0&date2=09%2F23%2F1862&searchType=advanced&language=&sequence=0&lccn=sn84024738&words=UPRISING&proxdistance=5&state=Virginia&rows=20&ortext=uprising&proxtext=&phrasetext=&andtext=&dateFilterType=range&page=1. (accessed September 9, 2013).

The National Gallery. Willem van de Velde,. London. http://www.nationalgallery.org.uk/artists/willem-van-de-velde. (accessed September 11, 2013).

U.S. Army. Army Doctrine Publication. *Army Leadership,* ADP 6-22. Washington DC: Army Chief of Staff, September 10, 2012.

U.S. Army. Army Doctrine Reference Publication. *Army Leadership,* ADRP 6-22. Washington DC: Army Chief of Staff, August 1, 2012.

U.S. Government Accountability Office. Report to Congressional Committees GAO-14-29, *Joint Military Education: Actions Needed to Implement DOD Recommendations for Enhancing Leadership Development.* Washington DC: October 2013. http://www.gao.gov/assets/660/658527.pdf (accessed December 8, 2013).

U.S. Joint Chiefs of Staff, *Information Operations,* Joint Publication 3-13. Washington DC: Joint Chiefs of Staff, November 27, 2012.

U.S. Joint Chiefs of Staff. *Public Affairs,* Joint Publication 3-61. Washington DC: Joint Chiefs of Staff, August 25, 2010.

U.S. President. Letter. *Sustaining U.S. Global Leadership: Priorities for 21st Century Defense.* Washington DC: Government Printing Office, January 3, 2012.

U.S. President. Policy. *National Security Strategy.* Washington DC: Government Printing Office, May 2010.

U.S. President. Speech. "Remarks by the President in Address to the Nation on Syria." Washington DC. http://www.whitehouse.gov/the-press-office/2013/09/10/remarks-president-address-nation-syria (accessed September 11, 2013).

Vergun, David. "Odierno Shares Views on Military's Relationship With Media." *Army News Service,* October 22, 2012. http://www.defense.gov/News/NewsArticle.aspx?ID=118282 (accessed September 25, 2013)

Williams, Pete. "Military, Media and Manipulation," *The Washington Post,* March 17, 1991. D1. http://search.proquest.com.ezproxy6.ndu.edu/docview/140385452?accountid=12686 (accessed October 2, 2013).

Williams, Pete. "The Press and the Persian Gulf War." *Parameters* XXI, no. 3 (Autumn 1991): 2-9. http://strategicstudiesinstitute.army.mil/pubs/parameters/Articles/1991/1991%20williams.pdf (accessed October 2, 2013).

Witty, Patrick. "Malcolm Browne: The Story Behind the Burning Monk," in the *Time Lightbox*. August 28, 2012. http://lightbox.time.com/2012/08/28/malcolm-browne-the-story-behind-the-burning-monk/#1 (accessed November 19, 2013).

Wright, Donald P., and Timothy R. Reese. *On Point II: Transition to the New Campaign*. Kansas: Combat Studies Institute Press, 2008.

Wright, Patrick. *Tank.* New York: Viking, 2000.